Twin Tips

A Guide for Twin Moms by a Twin Mom

Courtnie Adair

To order additional copies of this book, contact:
Xlibris
1-888-795-4274
www.Xlibris.com
Orders@Xlibris.com

ISBN: Softcover   978-1-7960-9593-7
       EBook   978-1-7960-9592-0

Print information available on the last page

Rev. date: 05/05/2020

My Story (You Can Skip This Part)

I may be one of the few people who really anticipated having twins from the get-go. My husband and I had a serious talk about it and were fully prepared to bring on multiples. How did I know? Well, for starters, both of my maternal great grandparents are twins. My great grandmother is a fraternal twin, which is genetic, and nobody knows if my great-grandfather was identical or fraternal. So, genetics played a role even though none of the subsequent generations had twins (until me). My other suspicion came from my ovulation days. I always had ovulation pain on both ovaries. That's not uncommon, I know, but I just had this *feeling*.

Anyway, my husband and I started doing the deed. Two months went by, and my cycle was erratic, so my doctor put me on medication to get that process going again. Birth control can really screw with your stuff. After two additional months of ovulation predictor kits (OPKs) and charting basal body temperature (BBT), my doctor prescribed the magical little bean called Clomid. I was on the lowest dosage and my doctor assured me that no twins shall be had. Ha! I later pointed out how wrong she was. Yes, I know I'm a beast. But I'm a *smug* beast.

The first try on Clomid was a failure. The second attempt on Clomid gave me my big fat positive pee stick. I couldn't believe it! I should have known that something was up because I got a positive at 3.5 weeks pregnant. Normally, it takes at least four weeks for there to be enough of the HCG hormone present in your urine to get a positive. We told some friends and family, everyone was ecstatic, and my mom wiggled her way into our first ultrasound appointment. At this point, I'm seven weeks along, just far enough to hear a heartbeat (or two… or three). Can you see where I'm going with this? The ultrasound screen turns on. There are clearly two amniotic sacs. My mom is squealing, I'm shouting about how I knew it all along, and my husband is bouncing on his heels.

The ultrasonographer is strangely quiet. She says something that makes my heart drop *hard*. "Wait, I think there's another one."

I'm in shock. Triplets? Holy shit.

The ultrasonographer calls the doctor in because she's never seen triplets. The doctor confirms that we have "a pair and a spare." We had started with fraternal twins, and one of those cheeky bastards decided to split into two identical twins. Then comes the bad news:

the single fraternal twin has a weak heartbeat. We're sent to a specialist the next day, and within 24 hours the heart had stopped beating. We were down to only identical twins and mourned the loss of our third little bean. Are we greedy people? Maybe. Would all three kids have survived a very difficult pregnancy? Maybe not. Silver linings are there for a reason. All in all, I thought I would have fraternal twins and I ended up with the less-likely identical twins. So, was I right? Technically. And that's all that matters.

We get through the first trimester without a hitch. Sure, I'm a bit nauseous, but it's really not that bad. The second trimester was the absolute worst for me. It's supposed to be this lovely time before you blow up like a balloon and you're not sick anymore. I, however, am cursed with disgusting, hormonal, pizza-face acne. Yes, I'm vain. When you've dealt with acne your whole teenage and adult life, you tend to feel demoralized about it. Well, I didn't fare very well in that second trimester and I was a little bit… touchy… about it. There's an old wives' tale about baby girls stealing your beauty when you're pregnant. I had my heart set on girls. For my entire life, I always pictured having daughters. I mean, what would I even do with a baby boy? My husband had the biggest, shit-eating grin on his face when the ultrasonographer told us we were having boys. I was dazed. At the time, I couldn't imagine raising sons. Now I wouldn't mind having nothing but sons. They're *amazing*. No regrets.

All in all, not a bad pregnancy until the 20th week anatomy scan. Of course, this was the scan that I invited my family to see. Do you remember what Murphy's Law is? If something can go wrong, it will? Yeah. I had waited months to invite my family because I was so worried about there being problems. Well, I'm informed during this visit that I had a shortening cervix, which is common in twin pregnancies. I'm put on bed rest and was to go back the next week for a follow-up scan. In the span of that week, my cervix shortened further and I started dilating. The doctor sat down with my husband and me, explaining how I was starting to go into labor and that the babies can't survive if they're born before 24 weeks. That was insanity. How could I be going into labor and not even know it? I felt fine! The doctor explained that there's a surgery option to keep the pregnancy going, a little something called a cerclage. It's basically a stitch on my lady parts to keep everything sealed tight. Of course, there's a possibility that the surgeon will accidentally break my water and send me into full-on labor. Terrifying, right? Well, we did it. It worked. I was put on bed rest for the rest of my pregnancy, which lasted a full 35 weeks. All of my doctors were pessimistic and didn't think I'd make it to 30 weeks, much less an extra month. When I want something done, I'm pretty tenacious about it. I wanted my babies to be at least five pounds at birth, and that's exactly what I got. Sure, my body almost drowned itself (good ol' preeclampsia – a complication characterized by high blood pressure and signs of damage to another organ system, most often the liver and kidneys), and my organs were shutting down by the end, but hey, I'm sitting here typing this book with an eight-month-old baby on my lap. A baby who only took a 20-minute nap, despite my best efforts. Turd. Don't worry, his brother is napping soundly. This story has a happy ending.

You're still reading this? I'm shocked. I guess I could tell you about their birth. The rest of the pregnancy was mostly uneventful. I got big. As someone who has always been a tiny person, this was a new experience for me. I had to buy a whole new wardrobe (shopping is the worst). I monitored how much weight I was gaining because I had heard about preeclampsia. Women who are pregnant with multiples are at a higher risk for it. Essentially, doctors don't know the exact cause of preeclampsia, but the only cure is ~~more cowbell~~ to deliver the baby.

Preeclampsia can prevent the placenta from receiving enough blood and cause a host of issues for both the baby and mom. Typical symptoms include sudden weight gain, headaches, and protein in your urine. There are other symptoms, of course, but these are the main ones that I was told to look out for. I knew something was up when I started gaining weight *fast*. I told my doctor that I suspected the worst, and she assured me that I had no other symptoms and didn't have preeclampsia (strike two, Doctor). I was told "You're just pregnant with twins" over and over…and over. I'll never mistrust my instincts again.

At that point, I'm almost 35 weeks along. I can't breathe when I lie down. "You're just pregnant with twins. They're crushing your lungs." I can't sleep at night. "You're just pregnant with twins. It's normal to be tired and lose sleep." I'm having chest pains. "You're just pregnant with twins. It's a common symptom." I give up on talking to my doctor and nurses. I tell my mom that I can't breathe or sleep, and she pushes me to try one more time with my OB's office. I send a quick email on Sunday night, and the nurse replies the next morning, saying that I can get checked out at my local ER, just in case. I drag my feet the whole way, complaining that they're going to send me home with the advice that I'm "just pregnant with twins." It may have started out that way in the ER, but boy were those doctors surprised by my bloodwork and scans. No amount of *Grey's Anatomy* could have prepared me to understand doctor-speak, but basically my organs were beginning to shut down, and my lungs were filled with fluid. Water was also gathering around my heart, but I didn't know about that until a few days later (complications, yay!). The ER doctor had been so convinced that nothing was going to be wrong with me that she gave me the okay to eat lunch right before we received my results. Lo and behold, the ER doc consulted with my OB, and I was scheduled for a C-section that night (eight hours later, of course, because I had just eaten).

The day was finally here. My husband rushed over to the hospital from work. Personally, I didn't want a bunch of family in the waiting room. Visiting hours were going to be over by the time the boys were born, and I wanted to have skin to skin with my babies and spend alone time with them before the zombie horde of relatives descended upon us all. Well, I didn't get that. I caved to my husband's millionth request to text everyone while we were waiting. My fault, I know. Once they were pulled out of me, the nurse asked if I wanted to let the family see the boys before they were asked to go home. Drugged, tired and just a little confused, I said sure, and there they went. The boys had to go to the NICU (Neonatal Intensive Care Unit) right after that, so I only got to see them for a few minutes in the recovery room. Oh, well. Live and learn. Two days later, I had to go to the operating room one more time. My doctor removed a liter of blood clots that were keeping my wounds from closing. Following a blood transfusion and several thousand blood draws, my arm looked like a meth dealer's most loyal customer. I loathe needles, but I'd do it again to bring those nuggets into the world. We all went home after five days in the hospital, and that was that.

Later, a friend asked me if I had one of those overly sentimental moments when I first saw my children. Um….no. I never had that moment where angels sing and the hand of God engulfs you in the warm and fuzzies. What I felt was more of a sense of rightness. It felt like this was exactly where I was supposed to be, holding my boys and then passing them off to dad to change dirty diapers. I love being a mom. It gives me an ultimate sense of purpose. Yes, twins are hard. Children are hard in general, whether you have one or five. Now that my kids are becoming a little more independent and I have a small amount of free time, I've decided to write this book. From conception to a year old, I have tips and tricks that I hope will make your life easier. At a minimum, my goal is to give you some peace of mind. It will be okay. You can do this. And hey, if Ellen wants me on her show to talk about this book, oh darn. Twist my arm.

Congrats!

You're a baller! On average, women will try for six months before succeeding in getting pregnant. Look at you, you overachiever! Not only do you have two little nuggets preciously stealing your nutrients and energy, but you're going above and beyond by reading this book. You're going to be a great mom. Just breathe. I know it is overwhelming, but twins are amazing and so are you. Don't let anyone kill your vibe. You're going to get "advice" like "You'll never sleep again" or "You'll never have sex again" or "You'll never be this skinny again." Ignore these people (I'm looking at you, Aunt Helen!). You will sleep. You will have sex. You will lose that baby weight. Sure, it may take some time for these things to happen, but they WILL happen.

I don't know if anyone's told you this, but getting pregnant can be really freaking hard. Like not *The Handmaid's Tale* kind of hard but also not *Juno* kind of easy. Consider yourself a mudblood because you're basically capable of doing magic (especially if your twins are identical). So how does this happen? How do you get the BOGO deal? I can assure you, the whole thing is your fault. Only the mom can cause multiple babies to pop out. There are two types of twins – fraternal and identical. Fraternal twins have different DNA strands. They start as two separate eggs that are fertilized by two separate sperm. Thus, you can have two totally different babies. Normally, a woman only releases one egg per ovulation cycle, but it's very possible to spit out more (one egg per ovary or even two eggs from one ovary). Identical twins are magically split into two babies from one egg and one sperm. Science hasn't yet solved the mystery of identical twins, and there is no confirmed theory about why it happens. See? Magic. Your Hogwarts letter must have gotten lost. Identical twins share the same DNA and are almost always the same gender. Whether fraternal or identical, your two little squirts are already very special.

Each type of twin has a different set of complications. Now, I don't want you to fret over the what-ifs. Yes, things can go wrong. Things can also go right. I was told that my twins would be born before seven months, but they cooked for a full eight months. Don't be discouraged. When I began writing this book, I had every intention to talk about possible complications during the pregnancy. However, as I'm trying to piece together the information, I'm getting super bummed out. If that's how I feel about it, how is it going to make you feel? Reading the information doesn't mean it's going to come true for you. Being pregnant is stressful enough as it is, and there is no point in scaring you with the "what-ifs." I'm going to leave those discussions between you and your doctor. If you'd like online resources for this topic, please see the Online Resources section of this book. Let's move on to happier subjects.

Now that you've confirmed your twin pregnancy, when is the right time to tell the world? That's totally up to you. The age of viability is 24 weeks. This means that the babies can survive on their own (with medical assistance) after 24 weeks of gestation. Twenty-four weeks is a long time to wait. That's closer to the end of the second trimester. I wouldn't blame you if you wanted to spread your gospel sooner, and it's completely understandable if you'd like to wait until everything is just right. The risk of a miscarriage drops around 12 weeks (the end of the first trimester). I know many moms who chose to announce at that point. My husband and I waited until 13 weeks to announce our babies on social media. For my next pregnancy, I'm going to wait until after the anatomy scan, which is roughly around 20 weeks. I say that now, but who knows if I'm going to stick to my guns. Pregnancy is an exciting and scary thing. Of course we want to brag about it!

It was the Hormones, Baby.

By the time you're ready to tell the world, you'll probably be "feeling" your pregnancy pretty strongly. Don't worry about having double or worse symptoms than your singleton mom counterparts. Every pregnancy is different. With my boys, I vomited a whopping three times. Sure, I was nauseous occasionally, but it wasn't that bad. One of my best friends couldn't keep down her breakfast on any given day, and she "only" had one kiddo cooking. We are all different with hormones raging in a variety of directions. So, let's talk about some of the symptoms that you MIGHT experience and when:

First trimester: 1 to 13 weeks
Second trimester: 14 to 27 weeks
Third trimester: 28 to 40 weeks

Sore breasts: All three trimesters. Relief can sometimes be found with a more supportive bra, looser clothing, doctor-approved pain meds (like Tylenol), and cold or hot compresses.

Excessive hunger: All three trimesters. I was absolutely starving during my first trimester. I couldn't go more than two hours without eating a snack. Eat when you're hungry but make your snacks and meals as healthy as possible.

Darker nipples: All three trimesters. Yeah, this is a weird one. Your body is gearing up to tackle breastfeeding.

Dizziness: All three trimesters. Please, please, please make sure to drink enough water. At least 8 glasses per day, according to the American Pregnancy Association.

Fatigue: All three trimesters. There's not much to say about this one. Drink water, get some sleep, and rest when needed. I know, that's easier said than done (especially if you've got another little terrorist running around).

Bleeding: First trimester. Talk to your doctor about any spotting. If you experience heavier bleeding than spotting, call your doctor immediately.

Cramping: All three trimesters. Doctor-approved painkillers can help too.

Nausea and/or vomiting: First trimester. I'm sure you're shocked by this one. It may be called "morning sickness," but I assure you, it's not limited to the morning. You might find relief with vitamin B-6 supplements, ginger-based products, eating small meals more frequently, and sucking on sweet candy (such as Jolly Ranchers). Your doctor can prescribe anti-nausea medication, as well. Timing your prenatal vitamin pill differently might also help. Try taking it when you feel the least sick since the iron in the pill can exacerbate nausea. Oh, and you don't have to take twice the vitamins with twins. One serving is sufficient.

Mood swings: All three trimesters. You're not crazy, your hormones are crazy. There's a difference.

Dry eyes: All three trimesters. Dehydration or a decrease in tear-duct production can cause dry eyes. You may need to keep eye drops handy, wear glasses instead of contacts, and forego makeup for the time being. Nothing makes you feel better than looking like a four-eyed zombie, am I right?

Hemorrhoids: Third trimester. Oof, this one's a doozy. Pressure from your growing uterus can put pressure on veins, causing them to swell. There's not much that you can do to prevent this, just try not to strain while pooping. If you're having issues, take stool softening supplements.

Food aversions/cravings: All three trimesters. I may or may not have eaten a grilled cheese for breakfast every day during my second trimester. I also used my "do not use" credit card that my husband didn't know about to buy Taco Cabana for lunch three times a week. Don't judge me. Your body tends to tell you what it needs, confusing as it may be. Cravings aren't something you need to be concerned about, unless you want something you shouldn't be eating (like paper or dirt).

Nasal Congestion: All three trimesters. Allergies and the increase in blood flow might be the culprit for your mucus problems. There are doctor-approved allergy medicines to help you find relief.

Acne: All three trimesters. Oh, hormones, how I hate you. Does it help if I say pregnancy acne is only temporary? The best practice is to not touch it. Gently wash your face daily (or twice daily). Everybody's skin is different, so you do you.

Constipation: All three trimesters. Eat your fiber, kids. Iron supplements can contribute to constipation. Drink plenty of water and ask your doctor about over-the-counter supplements (like stool softeners). Did you hear about the constipated accountant? He couldn't budget.

Bloating and Gas: All three trimesters. The hormone called progesterone is the instigator for your gas problems. Don't worry, it was the babies; not you.

Increased urination: All three trimesters. This will probably get worse as the babies grow and press on your bladder. You may even pee yourself when laughing. I won't tell anyone if you don't tell anyone.

Shortness of breath: Third trimester. A word of caution regarding this symptom. If you are in your third trimester and have trouble breathing, especially when lying down, please discuss it with your doctor. When this happened to me, it was because I had severe Preeclampsia and my lungs were filling with water. That may not necessarily happen to you, just be careful.

Swollen feet/ankles: Second and third trimesters. Sudden swelling in the face or hands can also be a sign of preeclampsia, but it's very common in the feet and ankles. Prop your feet up, exercise, and drink plenty of water. I promise this will go away very quickly once your little nuggets are born. You may still experience some joint pain afterwards. Just give it time. I had pain in my right ankle until my boys were about seven months old.

Stretch marks: Second and third trimesters. There are belly creams that claim to prevent stretch marks, but science hasn't confirmed it. You aren't guaranteed to suffer from stretch marks just because you have twins. Personally, I used a belly cream every day and my stretch marks are minimal.

Linea nigra: Second and third trimesters. No, this is not an insult. It's literally a brown vertical line that develops along your belly. Do we know the cause? Nope. It will most likely disappear within a few months after your babies are born, but there's a chance that it'll be a permanent reminder of your woman warrior status. I'm currently nine months postpartum, and I can still see a faint line. Oh, well. I'm going to look fabulous in those one-piece bathing suits.

Fake contractions: Second and third trimesters. These are called Braxton Hicks contractions. It's your body's way of preparing itself for the real thing. If you're not sure if your contractions are phonies, just drink some water, eat a snack, go to the bathroom, and see if the contractions come at regular intervals. If they're Braxton Hicks contractions, they'll be irregular and go away.

Sciatic nerve pain: All three trimesters. Some women can find relief through massage and stretching. Swimming can also help.

Nose bleeds: First trimester. This is caused by extra blood circulating throughout your body, including your nose.

Swollen/bleeding gums: All trimesters. Pregnant women are more susceptible to gum disease, so make sure you brush and floss!

Gagging on your toothbrush: First trimester. This can often be the first sign of pregnancy. Using a smaller toothbrush (like a children's toothbrush) might help.

Tingling hips when lying down: Second and third trimesters. As your uterus grows, it puts pressure on your nerves. Try stretching and changing sleeping positions often.

Charley horse: Second and third trimesters. It's a fancy name for a muscle spasm. Ever had severe cramping in your calves? Yep, that's a charley horse. I found that stretching my calves before bedtime helped a lot. That, and drinking water.

Heartburn: Second and third trimesters. Hmmm, I wonder what could cause this. Oh, right: hormones. Progesterone relaxes the valve between your esophagus and stomach, allowing stomach acid to creep back up your esophagus. Gross, right? Just keep those Tums handy.

You may have noticed that these symptoms are all the same as singleton pregnancies. Isn't being a human incubator fun? Even better, these symptoms can come and go as they please. There is no guarantee of when or how bad they will get. Oh, and here's a side note – Your partner, no matter how compassionate, may not understand what you're going through. Some people have a really hard time with understanding what they can't see or experience for themselves. My husband is one of these people. I could say that I'm nauseous, and he'd only make jokes about me being sick of him. If you think it'll do some good, ask your partner to read a book about pregnancy (Maybe this one? Eh? Eh?), do some online research, or at least refrain from being insensitive. Sometimes, that's all you can hope for. There are a lot of wonderful partners out there who go above and beyond for their women. Sit down, have a conversation, maybe take the time to write out what you're feeling if you have trouble articulating your problems out loud. Try to communicate in a positive way. Yes, you're pregnant, but remember that your partner is going through a stressful time too. After all, someone must make you that grilled cheese sandwich at 5 a.m. The Dad abides.

Bed Rest

Not all doctors agree on prescribing bed rest when multiples are involved. If you're having a healthy pregnancy, you most likely won't be put on bed rest. When I started going into labor at 20 weeks (due to a shortened cervix), I went on bed rest and didn't get out of it for the rest of the pregnancy. Bed rest doesn't mean that you must literally lay in bed for 24 hours per day. I mostly reclined on my couch and worked from home on my laptop. I was told not to walk long distances, no exercising, and to stay within thirty minutes of our hospital. Best of all, the doctor kept repeating "pelvic rest." My husband and I nodded, thinking he just meant that I needed to stay off of my feet. Nope. He clarified that we were not to have sex under any circumstances. We laughed, and then my husband cried about it at home. It was a long four months for him. If you are put on bed rest and need some ideas to stay busy, here you go:

- Work from home
- Write a book
- Adult coloring
- Crosswords, Sudoku, or other puzzles
- Snuggle with the closest warm body
- Watch all 14 seasons of *Supernatural*
- Watch all 17 seasons of *Grey's Anatomy* (disclaimer: there may be more seasons by the time you read this)
- Facebook stalk that girl you hated in high school
- Plan your baby shower
- Make voodoo dolls
- Hide voodoo dolls
- Plan Christmas gifts
- Crochet or sew
- Create a Pinterest board for your second and third weddings

If you're still going crazy after all of these activities, you can also balance your checkbook. That'll keep you busy and entertained for hours.

The BOGO Deal: Fake News

Let's talk about something that is near and dear to my heart as a CPA. Babies are expensive. Like, hella expensive. While I joke that twins are a buy-one-get-one-free deal, you do, in fact, have to pay more for a twins delivery. You will be charged for both babies and many doctors prefer a C-section, which is more costly than a natural delivery. Plus, you might need more ultrasounds with twins. My ultrasounds were $200 a pop, and I had a Cerclage surgery on top of that. My doctor's delivery fee alone was $2,800. That didn't include prenatal care, hospital fees, pediatrician fees, or the extra procedures I needed from complications. Luckily, my boys did not need to stay in the Newborn Intensive Care Unit (NICU). Speaking of the NICU, I highly recommend using a hospital with a Level IV NICU.

Twins are often born premature and sometimes need special attention. Here's a break-down of the different levels:

> Level I: Normal nursery care.
> Level II: Advanced care for sick and premature children.
> Level III: More intensive care for seriously ill newborns.
> Level IV: Round-the-clock care for newborns who need surgical options.

Yes, if used, the NICU will bring another level of costs. However, it's best to not need it yet have it than to need it and not have it. You want the best care possible, available 24/7.

Not only is childbirth insanely expensive in the United States, but most OB facilities require you to pay their fee in advance. I tried arguing against paying it up front because my cost was based on my insurance plan, deductible, and out-of-pocket maximum for the year even though the babies would be born in the following year (thus completely changing my bill). Not only that, but the cost is also dependent on who bills insurance first and if you meet your deductible or maximum out-of-pocket for the year. I lost the argument but won the war. They issued a refund check eventually for overcharging me. Despite my views on our healthcare system, insurance does cover a lot of the cost. However, there are other ways to save. A Health Savings Account (HSA) or a Flexible Spending Account (FSA) are major helpers with the babymaking industry. These accounts are provided by employers as a means to assist with medical costs. Essentially, pre-tax money is allocated to an account each month from your paycheck. Your employer may or may not also contribute to this account. You are allowed to use this money for a variety of medical purposes. Here are the basics:

HSAs:

- Roll over each year.
- Interest/earnings are tax free.
- Payments to qualifying medical costs are tax free.
- Portable from job to job.
- Funds are only available as you contribute to the account.

FSAs

- Use-it-or-lose-it. You have one year to spend the cash.
- Self-employed individuals are not eligible.
- Can also be spent on childcare.
- Payments to qualifying medical costs are tax free.
- You can access the lump sum immediately.

I like to view an HSA as a typical savings account that you put money into, while an FSA is more like a loan from your employer. If you have to choose between these two options or insurance, I would stick with insurance. An FSA or HSA should be used as an additional cost-saving resource, not an insurance replacement. Disclaimer: I don't know your specific financial information. My advice is general and might not be the right fit for you. Please make the best decision based on your personal situation.

Another way to reduce your cost is by fighting it. You will start to receive bills in the mail weeks to months after your babies arrive. I've managed to completely get rid of bills by calling and complaining. Yes, being a whiner can you ahead in life sometimes. If that doesn't work, most hospitals will accept payment plans. You won't know until you try. The answer is always no if you don't ask. Of course, you could also just move to Canada. I hear their childbirth deliveries cost less. What's a little snow, eh?

Here's another way to save: opt out of non-essential tests or procedures. Talk to your doctor about what's really needed. Here is a typical schedule of ultrasounds (although mothers of twins usually require more attention and thus more ultrasound exams):

- 8 weeks. By the way, this is a wand up the vag. The movies totally get this wrong by showing an over-the-belly ultrasound exam. How freakin' awkward if you invite family/friends to the first appointment. This is the appointment that confirms your pregnancy and initial viability (you get to hear the heartbeats!). If you already know you're pregnant with twins, you'll probably have already gone through this process.
- 12 weeks. Another ultrasound to determine viability.
- 16 weeks. This ultrasound is optional and may not be covered by insurance. You can elect to find out your babies' sex by now. There is also a blood test that can tell you the sex even earlier, but that may be more expensive. If you're having fraternal twins, the blood test will not be your best option. The test searches for male chromosomes from Mom's blood. Fraternal twins could be either gender, so if you test positive for a boy under the hood, you could still have a girl, too. However, if you test positive for a girl, you can rest assured that both babies are ~~the superior gender~~ ladies.
- 20 weeks. This is an in-depth anatomy scan. Your babies' organs will be examined to make sure everything is developing right.
- 36 weeks. As you near your due date, your babies will be checked for any last-minute complications. If you've elected to deliver vaginally, your doctor will check to make sure the twins' heads are down.

Some doctors specialize in natural delivery for twins. It's riskier, and you should prepare yourself for the possibility of a C-section anyway, but a natural delivery could put a dent in the expense bucket. Plus, the recovery is easier with a natural delivery. If you don't have help after your babies are born, this may be the best option for you. Side note: If you go through with a natural delivery, you WILL poop on the table. It's not a twins thing, just a childbirth thing. There's no need to be embarrassed. Own it!

Don't forget about a baby shower. Your friends and family will most likely want to be involved, and there's no better way to support you than by providing clothes, furniture, diapers, etc. Cloth diapers could be a cheaper option, but remember that you already have your hands full with those two nuggets and cloth diapers require a lot of washing. If money's not an issue, you can pay to have your cloth diapers picked up, washed, and delivered. After your kiddos are born, you can buy in bulk (Hello, Costco!) and make your own baby food (but who has time for that?). Don't be afraid to use hand-me-downs. Some of your local businesses may have discounts for twin parents too.

Twiniversity.com is an amazing tool to find deals and special events. Ask your pediatrician for discounts or freebies on formula too. The cost of formula can get crazy when you're feeding two.

Yes, twins cost more no matter what you do. It will be okay. Just take it one day at a time and start couponing!

The Yum Yums and No Nos

Okay, so all of that may seem pretty negative. Let's highlight something positive: You get to EAT! If you are starting at a healthy BMI, twice the baby means twice the calories (starting in the second trimester). Your little baby beans are too tiny in the first trimester to require more calories from you. You need roughly 300 extra calories per fetus per day in the second trimester. That translates to 600 delicious calories for you, mama bear. Bump that up to 900 calories in the third trimester. If your BMI (body mass index) is below or above average, you may need to adjust your caloric intake. Talk to your doctor about what's best for you. Of course, "eating more" doesn't mean "eating more junk." You'll need a healthy mix of protein, vegetables and fruit. Be careful about your sugar intake and remember that fruit contains a lot of sugar too. Moms who are pregnant with twins are more likely to develop gestational diabetes. I recommend weighing yourself once a week (at the same time and on the same day for consistency) to monitor any excessive eating. You can also use online weight gain calculators to see if you're in a healthy ballpark for pregnancies. I've included the link to *babycenter.com*'s estimator, which I liked and used frequently, in the online resources section. Diet restrictions for twins are the same as singleton pregnancies. No alcohol, drugs, and worst of all, no sushi. Here's a list of things to avoid or minimize:

- Fish with a lot of mercury (swordfish, king mackerel, tuna, shark, Chilean sea bass, lobster, and Alaskan cod). You can still eat other types of cooked fish that contain omega-3 fatty acids, such as shrimp and salmon. The FDA recommends that pregnant women eat at least eight ounces of seafood per week. If you love sushi, you don't have to give it up completely. Order tempura rolls and pig out.
- Deli meat can contain a bacteria called listeria, which is dangerous for both you and your babies. Pregnant women are more susceptible to infection. If you crave deli meats like I did, you can safely eat it if the meat is heated enough to steam. At that point, any listeria bacteria is eliminated.
- Raw eggs and sprouts put you at risk for salmonella. Take raw cookie dough and brownie mix off the menu, for now.
- Caffeine can be consumed in limited quantities. The American Pregnancy Association recommends drinking less than 200 mg per day. Remember that other drinks/foods besides coffee contain caffeine, such as tea, soda, and chocolate.
- Unpasteurized milk and cheese can carry a host of bacteria. Luckily, many dairy products in grocery stores are pasteurized.

Eating healthy can be difficult on a normal day, but it's especially important now. I knew a mother who ate cooked meats and veggies first, then junk food and sugar if she was still hungry afterwards. Your babies will taste whatever you taste through the amniotic fluid, so you can never start too early on letting them experience a variety of flavors. Whatever you eat now could affect what they like to eat after they're born. Crazy, right?

Here's something that got on my nerves every single day – people love to comment on a pregnant woman's weight. Even if the comment is positive, it's still a reminder that you're getting bigger. Many people told me, "You don't even look pregnant from behind!" which just made me more paranoid about how I looked from the front. With hormones racing, sensitivity levels soar to new heights. If you experience this, try not to let it get you down (I know, easier said than done). Some people have good intentions and don't understand why you may take it a different way. Other people are just mean and need to mind their own damn business. Here are some of my favorite come-backs for those people who need a good smackdown:

- Would it be okay if I borrow some clothes from you soon?
- What? I'm not pregnant. (I can't tell you how much I loved using this one on strangers who overstep).
- I've got two. What's your excuse?
- Am I gaining too much? Well, I'm doing as much cocaine as I can to offset it. I guess it's not working.
- Dieting is for ugly people.
- Shall I tell your loved ones that those were your final words?

Of course, you could just go with the classic "fuck off." That one never fails. Once, while I was checking out at the grocery store, the cashier made a face and said, "You've got a big baby." I was wearing a shirt that clearly said twins were coming. I guess she was too distracted by my big fat belly to read. Oh, and God forbid if anyone tries to touch your belly without consent. I didn't mind it so much once there was actual movement to feel, but any touching before that was just hella awkward. If you didn't put it there, don't touch it. There are these amazing Kevlar vests sold on Amazon that will keep people at bay for a little while. Once, when my mother-in-law wouldn't stop touching me (before there was even a bump), I grabbed her belly in retaliation. It backfired big time, as she GIGGLED AND SAID TO DO IT AGAIN. I will never, ever touch another person's belly for the rest of my life.

You may be wondering when you're going to show. It's entirely possible that you'll show earlier than a singleton pregnancy. Your pants could feel tighter at the end of the first trimester, or you won't notice any changes until you're closer to four months pregnant. Every woman has a different body style, and there's no hard rule on when people will be able to notice you've got two buns in the oven.

Baby(ies) Shower

You're probably wondering if you need two of everything. Nope, you sure don't. Here's a list of things you WILL need to double up on:

- Bassinets: Things might be easier on you to put the twins in bassinets in your room, especially if you're having a C-section. Sharing a bed is not safe and not recommended, especially once the snuggle buddies start moving around. I bought a twin-sized pack 'n play with double bassinets on top. The boys were able to still see each other and touch hands with mesh between them. So freaking cute.

- Cribs, mattresses, mattress protectors, and crib sheets: There's no hard and fast rule on when to move your babies to a crib. You could use cribs immediately, wait until they're almost too big for their bassinets (around three months, roughly), or just move them into cribs when you're ready. If you need to save money now, you could buy cribs later on. Just remember that you'll have to make time to put them together, which could be a challenge. The more expensive cribs can also transition into a toddler's bed later.
- Baby blankets
- Clothes: Easy is best. People are going to buy the cutest, most frustrating clothes to put on your child. Those super adorable three-piece outfits from Target will make you pull your hair out. Dressing two squirming kids can be a pain. At night, I always liked zip up pajamas better than snap-ons. Babies scratch themselves, too. Some pajamas come with sleeves that cover their hands like mittens. Socks are a must. I still haven't put shoes on my boys (they're ten months at this point). Shoes aren't recommended anymore. People use to think it helped kids learn to walk, but now science says barefoot is best to help the muscles grow.
- Diapers: Want to hear a poop joke? Never mind, it's too corny. There are many different brands of diapers and they're basically all the same with small differences. Don't feel bad about asking for different brands to see what you like.
- Pacifiers
- Formula: Even if you plan on purely breastfeeding, have a little formula available. Different types of formula will be useful if you have a picky eater (or two).
- Bibs: We learned quickly that some bibs are better than others. Once the child learns how to yank on them, the scratchy Velcro bibs will be the enemy. Ouchy.
- Double seat stroller: I currently have four strollers. One double stroller that fits the click-in car seats, one side-by-side stroller that's easier to get into the car (but the kids needed to learn to control their necks first to use it), and two single-child strollers. There's an occasion for each one. Do you need four? Nope. If you can only pick one, go with the big double stroller that fits the car seats. You'll use it the most in the first three months.
- Car seats (duh): Like I mentioned before, try to get the car seats that click into the double stroller. There are also car seats that will last until the kids are old enough to sit without assistance, but those are more expensive.
- Car seat toys: These aren't totally necessary, but it's cool to have hanging toys on the car seat. It occupies them for long car rides.
- Seat mirrors: You can strap a mirror to the headrest. A quick look in your rearview mirror will tell you how the kids are doing.
- Bottles, caps and nipples: I used an Ameda pump, but Medela bottles are superior. Luckily, they're compatible. You can get their bottles/caps/nipples on Amazon and in most stores. Your babies will drink very little at first, but they'll increase their fluid intake quickly. You'll probably need 8 oz. bottles around four months. Unless you like punishing yourself, you'll want the bottles that are dishwasher safe.

- Burp cloths: These are basically just soft rags that cost twice as much. If it has to do with babies, expect a price surge.
- Swaddles: Oh, my goodness, I loved our little baby burritos. They're just so cute when they're all wrapped up and sucking on binkies.
- Swings: Okay, maybe you don't need two swings, but I sure did. My nuggets practically lived in them for the first month. They stopped liking them around four months or so.
- Binky leashes: I found out about these several months too late. They're basically clips with a rope around the pacifier. You clip it onto your kid and voila, no more lost binkies.
- Wipes: Costco sells them in bulk. I'm sure other stores do, too, but I'm a loyal customer and no one is taking my Costco away from me.
- Teething toys: Even if only one baby is teething, the other might get jealous if they don't get a special toy, too.

Here's another list of things you might want, but don't need two of:

- Baby monitor: One attribute I recommend splurging for is a monitor that swivels remotely. I get annoyed every day because my camera isn't angled enough to see both kids.
- Infant acetaminophen and Benadryl: Talk to your pediatrician about proper dosages.
- Body carrier: There are backpack carriers and wraps that cocoon the baby to your body.
- Breastfeeding pillow
- Boobie pads: I'm talking about the lactation pads for leaking breasts. You are definitely going to want these.
- Nipple cream: The first few weeks of breastfeeding and pumping are rough.
- Pump: Even if you plan on putting them on the breast, get one free through insurance! During the first three months, you will need to pump in addition to natural breastfeeding. When choosing a pump, the main differences are closed vs open pumping system. Closed systems have a barrier between your milk and the pump that prevents contamination (in both your milk and the pump). If milk gets in the pump, it will be a bitch to clean. If bacteria gets in your milk, it can lead to problems with your babies. Medela is probably the most recognizable pumping brand, but if you need to buy any pump parts or a whole second pump, their equipment is expensive. I used Medela in the hospital and my Ameda pump at home. I liked Ameda because everything was available on Amazon at a way cheaper price, so I bought a second pump just in case my first one crapped out. It never did.
- Bottle brush and drainer board
- Highchair that leans back: I didn't have one of these, and I wish I did. They're really great for letting your kids watch you while you cook or clean the dishes. You'll need two once they're older and eating solids, which starts at six months.
- Baby bath and wash: Until they can sit up on their own, it's really hard to bathe two kids at once. If you're determined, you could put them both on a flat surface and get it over with. My kids hated bathing anywhere except the tub. I think it had to do with cold drafts in the rest of the apartment.

- Baby towels. Trust me, they can share a towel. Actually, if you need to save some money, they can most likely use regular towels. Baby towels are softer, but it's not dire if you don't have any.
- Diaper pail: Oh, my lord, get one with a good lid. Ain't nobody gonna want to smell THAT. Okay, just one more poop joke. What's it called when your kid poops really fast? A ninja turdle.
- Diaper caddy: I had one for each room. They're just baskets that can hold diapers, diaper cream, wipes, etc. and they doubled as a toy when my kids got older. They love boxes and pulling things out of them. Putting things back in their assigned boxes wasn't as fun, though.
- Changing station, mattress and sheets: When you're changing two kids ten times a day, it can kill your back to hunch over on the floor. You don't want to change them where their pee missiles will make a mess. So, if you've got the cash or someone else is willing to buy one, a changing station is superb.
- Nursing cover
- Rocker or glider
- Laundry hamper
- Diaper bag: My "bag" is actually a backpack. One shoulder bags are really annoying to me. Plus, Dad didn't want to carry a big diaper purse.
- Carrier for your pumping stuff: Once again, I just used a backpack.
- Baby thermometer: They have the fancy ones that take temperature by touching your forehead or inside the ear, but mine never worked right. We just use the old-fashioned mouth ones. The forehead/ear ones are good for determining if a baby has a fever, but it's not the most accurate.
- Sound machine
- Outlet plug covers and gates: These can wait until the babies are up and moving.
- Baby gates: It made my life so much easier to put a giant gate around our living room. The boys had plenty of room for shenanigans and I could rest easily.
- Baby bouncer: I hardly used this, but lots of other moms love bouncers.
- Jumper: This could look like a stationary walker that lets your babies jump inside, or it could be a doorway jumper that also doubles as a swing. You won't need these for a few months. My kids became interested in our jumper around four months old, but they would only stay in it for a few minutes.
- Walker: You really won't want this until after six months, possibly later. Some moms never use them. Research has suggested that walkers inhibit a child's ability to learn to walk because they're not developing the right muscles or balance. They're also not safe if you have stairs, a pool, or anything else your child can fall into.
- Baby gym: Some kids love them, some kids don't. Mine became interested in our gym around four months old. My niece was fascinated with hers from the time she was born. To each their own, I guess.
- Disinfectant wipes: It's so much easier to wipe down certain items than washing everything with water and soap. To get rid of any residue, you can wipe your item again with a baby wipe afterwards.

- Clothing drawers: whether you have a dresser or use closet bins, you need the storage space.
- Binder: a good organizational binder is perfect for storing vaccine records, doctor visits, birth certificates, and SSN cards.
- Blackout curtains
- Clorox wipes: Not for the babies! When you need to clean a counter or toy in a hurry, Clorox wipes are awesome. Moms don't always have time for soap and water. If it's a toy, you can do a second wipe with a baby wipe to get rid of any residue.

Okay, I love lists. The next list is full of items that I recommend not getting at all:

- Bottle warmer: If your water gets hot fast out of the faucet, it'll be easier just to fill a cup with hot water and set the bottle in it.
- Wipes warmer: I used one for a long time before calling it quits. Some babies have difficulty using regular temperature wipes after experiencing the warm ones, but my boys didn't seem to care either way.
- Stuffed animals: Hello, dog toys and choking hazards.
- Cute but impractical clothing. This includes anything with more than three buttons. Ain't nobody got time for that. Zippers are *amazing*.
- Peepee teepees: These are so dumb. They are little tents to put over boys' junk so that their pee doesn't get on you while you change them. They might work if your child stays totally still. Otherwise, one leg movement is all it takes to knock it off. I actually ended up using doggy pee pads instead. If you lay your kiddo on one and he or she pees, the pad soaks it up. That was way easier than constantly changing the sheets on the changing station cushion.
- Pacifiers with stuffed animals attached: If you have a dog, these expensive little "must haves" become dog toys. My kids never even cared for the stuffed animals.
- Boogie wipes: Be brave. Use your finger. If boogers were currency, I'd have an in-ground pool by now.

There are other things you can request at your baby shower. For instance, you can set up a college fund and ask for contributions. A grocery delivery service subscription is super helpful. Any sort of cleaning, cooking, or laundry service will be a huge asset. If you know ahead of time that you'll need a babysitter on certain days, you could ask for sign ups. Whip out a calendar and see if anybody is available. There are monthly book subscriptions for children's books. One of my favorite gifts was a binder for important baby documents, like vaccination records and birth certificates. I hadn't thought of that and was super glad to receive it as a gift. Other unique gift ideas include scrapbooks, photography sessions, door signs that say to be quiet, and mommy spa treatments. Don't be afraid to ask for something out of the ordinary. You'd be surprised at how willing people are to give a helping hand to twin mommies.

An Afterthought

Sometimes, the worst part about a pregnancy is the people around you. It's those people who make your pregnancy about themselves. Whether it's a mom who throws a fit when you say you don't want her in the delivery room, or an uncle who wants you to invite his best friend's sister to your already overpopulated baby shower, there will always be THAT person who makes you want to scream. There are plenty of old biddies who complain that you aren't asking them for advice and then give a lecture on how different pregnancy and child rearing was in their day. If you struggled to get pregnant, you may get tired of hearing, "Back in my day, we just did it." The older generation wasn't on birth control for ten years before trying to have a child. There were no fertility drugs. They didn't need to chart their BBT and undergo follicle scans. They may have good intentions. They may think they know what's best for you. They may talk shit to your spouse about how difficult you're being. Let me just say one thing: Fuck. Those. People. I don't care who they are or how they're related to you. You do not have to bow down to a single goddamn person. Stop caring about what your grandmother wants you to name your babies. Tell your family friend that you have more pressing worries than the baptism that's a year away (not to mention that a baptism is a personal and private choice between you and your significant other!). Send a PSA to the negative ninnies that you are not taking unsolicited advice at this time. This pregnancy is about YOU and YOUR PARTNER. No one else. They are your kids. People will try to take ownership of your children, as if you need to put their needs first. "This is MY first grandbaby, and I want to throw the baby shower!" Tell your mom "Too bad." Your best friend is hosting it at her house already. "I want to spend a week with you and MY NIECES since I'm not available during the rest of the year!" Oh, no. Sorry, Aunt Margaret. You are not staying with me the week after my C section just because it's convenient for you. "I know you're not letting HIM be a godparent over your Great-uncle Eli!" Yes, Dad, I am, because my husband's childhood friend has been with us from the beginning and doesn't just call when he wants money. Don't let these people fool you. They're not looking out for you. They're not "just being supportive." If anyone buys something for you, does something for you, or insists on inserting themselves into your pregnancy in any way that YOU DIDN'T ASK FOR OR WANT and then DEMANDS that you adhere to their expectations, that person is not supportive. They're manipulative. They're selfish. It's not a gift, it's a bribe. Raise your children how you want, and if anyone is stressing you out, take a step back and limit your interaction with them until after the babies are born. I know, it may seem harsh, but you're at risk for a premature birth already. Stress can make things worse. Focus on yourself, your babies, and your partner. Maybe even let your partner play defense to all of those people who are trying to get at you. Close your eyes and breathe. Those other people will melt away soon, and if they don't, I will personally come light them on fire for you. Let's see how they like the flames of war.

Independence Day

Okay, time's up. You're ready. Whether they're cutting or ripping their way out, all three of you are about to gain your independence and form trade alliances. Things are about to get lit.

As I'm not a "real mom" who delivered naturally, I can't tell you what to expect from a vaginal delivery. I've done a little research, though, and I'll try my best to prepare you for certain possibilities. There's a chance that your doctor will recommend that you give birth in an operating room. That way, the doctor can perform an emergency C-section (if required). The room might have more people than a typical delivery. Each child will have his or her own team of nurses and doctors upon ~~escape~~ arrival. Two fetal monitors will be used instead of one, for obvious reasons. Apparently, there is an external and internal fetal monitor, so you could technically use both kinds at once. Huh. Who knew?

Certain things will be the same as a singleton delivery. You can still have an epidural (yippee!). You will still poop on the table, maybe twice as much. If you're wondering why women poop on the table, it's because you're pushing with all of your might, but you can't feel anything below your belly button. In essence, it's all or nothing.

Every delivery is different. Having twins does not guarantee a long delivery. You won't know until it happens, so relax. Don't worry about it. I once knew a coworker whose wife delivered their baby in their bathtub. It was their second child and she went into labor at midnight. She knew what was coming, went into the bathroom, and *whoosh!* Out came the baby. Craaaaazy.

If you're having a C-section, I'll try to prepare you as best as I can. You'll get to the hospital and do all of your check-ins. Hopefully, you've already done the paperwork and they can go straight to poking you with needles. They'll put in an IV, check for heartbeats and baby positions, and maybe ask you if you want your tubes tied. Your partner should be allowed to stay with you for most of the prep work and surgery. They'll roll you into the operating room where several nurses and one or two anesthesiologists will start doing their thang. The epidural will be inserted into your lower back along your spine. This sounds worse than it actually is. It stings a little as the needle goes in and there's pressure, but it's no worse than suffering through an IV. For me, they instructed me to hunch over and hold a nurse's hand while a student inserted the epidural. It took a little longer than necessary. And by "a little," I mean that I was ready to rip off that student's arms and beat him with them. The epidural is worth it, though. You'll lay down and let everyone else do the work. Hopefully, they'll talk to you and help you to relax. Your hands will be strapped down, and a curtain will be put up between your head and your belly. They'll test the epidural to make sure it's working. Mine was tested with cold stimuli. If I could feel that a sponge was cold, more anesthesia was needed. The surgeon will enter the room and talk to you and your partner, making sure you're both okay. Once everything is just right, your doctor will begin the C-section. I can't tell you exactly what happens here as I'm not a doctor and I didn't see it for myself, but I'm assuming the doctor uses a scalpel, cuts past muscle and tissue and whatever else keeps your body together, and gently pulls your first baby out. You may feel some pressure before the kiddos are pulled out. Once they've made their getaway, you might also feel a sudden weight lifted. I know I did. I felt like I had been on a long, uphill hike with a backpack full of rocks and suddenly I was able to put that backpack down. The relief was staggering.

"Look, Mom! It's [insert baby's name]!" Whoa. Insane. That's a REAL LIVE BABY. LIKE, AN ACTUAL HUMAN. IT WAS INSIDE OF ME AND NOW IT'S NOT. WHAT THE ACTUAL FUCK.

Side note: Your babies may not look human. Twins are usually born premature, which means they're smaller and have less fat. My boys looked like little hairy troll men. Everyone kept saying how cute they were, and I applauded their lying skills. It's okay to think your babies are cute, ugly, fat, skinny, whatever. As long as you love them, you're good.

The nurse will take Baby A to be checked out. "Look, Mom! It's [insert second baby's name]!" Woooooooooooow. TWO BABIES! Congratulations, you're not pregnant anymore!

The nurses and pediatrician will check out Baby B. If everything is hunky dory, you may be able to have a few minutes of skin-to-skin time, which means that the babies will lay on your chest to bond. Then, they'll go to NICU while the doctor stitches you back up. You and your partner can decide beforehand where your partner will go. Will he/she stay with you, or go with the babies to the NICU? I told my husband to go with the babies. He found me afterwards in the recovery room, post-surgery. Once I was cleared from the recovery area, I was able to see my babies in NICU for a few moments. Our hospital had a mandatory policy for premature babies to stay in NICU for a few hours after birth. Your hospital may be different and your birth story will definitely be different. You may be able to keep your babies in your room with you, or you may not see them for a little while. If that's the case, just try to get some sleep. I know, that will be really hard when the nurses come by to check your vitals every few hours. Relax. You have a hard road ahead of you for the next eight weeks.

Here's where you need to talk to your partner about expectations. Do you let an avalanche of relatives and friends immediately come see you? Do you limit visitors to close relatives only? The only thing that I can tell you is that you will be emotional, tired, and hurting. It will be painful to cough, sneeze, or laugh. Anything that requires the use of your abs will be intolerable. Your first bathroom visit will be hell. Your insides will try to become outsides (or so it feels like). Do you want people to see you like that? Do you want all of the love and support that people will bring with them? Unless you change the babies on your bed, your partner will be doing most of the heavy lifting. Friends and family will be able to help just by holding your little troll men or women. Personally, I didn't mind visitors until my third day in the hospital. Things weren't going well for me due to blood loss. After finding out that I needed more scans, blood work, a blood transfusion, and another possible surgery, I told my husband that I didn't want to see anybody. He didn't relay this message and I burst into tears when my family surprisingly walked in. It made me feel bad, it made my family feel bad, and it made my husband feel bad. Your partner is going to be your advocate. He or she will stand between you, evil nurses, relatives, and friends. You both need to be on the same page. You matter more than parents, grandparents, best friends, or that third cousin who doesn't understand boundaries. Don't let anyone bully you into filling their expectations. Don't want to see them? You need your rest, end of story. You don't want anyone in the room while you learn how to breastfeed? That's your call. Kick everyone out. If your partner isn't keeping their end of the deal, you can discreetly ask your nurses to help get people to leave. I promise you, they've seen it all before.

If I could only give one piece of advice for a C-section delivery, it's to move around as soon as possible. Sitting still will make the pain horrendous later. Start small: wiggle your toes in the recovery room, shift your legs around, and scoot your booty in your bed as much as you can handle. Roll onto your side. Start attempting to sit up ASAP. It will be painful, but trust me, you don't want to stay still for too long. That was my biggest mistake. Due to all of my complications, I had an epidural in for three days, and I was stuck in bed the entire time. Nobody told me to move around, so I thought I was supposed to be immobile. Then, on the fourth day, a nurse came into my room and announced that they were removing my catheter, and I'd have to get up to use the restroom. Holy fuck, it was the most painful thing I've ever been through. It took a long time for me to make it three feet into the bathroom, and that was with both my husband and the nurse helping. However, it sucked a little bit less each time I got up. By the fifth day, I was walking along the hallway slowly, and with assistance. I went home that day. Most women are able to go home after three or four days. Once you're cleared for takeoff, steal as much stuff as you can. Yes, TAKE IT ALL. They're used to it. If you had a C-section, they will give you stomach wraps to keep everything tight. When I had to take mine off, I always felt like my guts were trying to spill out. Take as many of these wraps as you can. They'll also give you pacifiers, formula, baby diapers, and adult diapers. Yes, adult diapers. You will want these for the constant bleeding over the next few weeks. Our nurse said we could take anything we liked except the linens. Well, my husband went crazy over the cute duck blankets. His exact words: "They're DUCKS! On BABY BLANKETS! We must have them!" Yeeaaaah. He went a little nuts. Oh, well. We still have them.

The Spoils of War

There were many battles, but you won the war. Now it's time to return home to lick your wounds. Not literally. Please do not lick anything, you'll get an infection. This goes for your partner too. No licking.

Regardless of how you gave birth, your recovery time is roughly six weeks, maybe more. You will bleed throughout these weeks, getting rid of all the excessive blood that you accumulated during your time as a human incubator. Call your doctor if the bleeding increases or you pass clots larger than a quarter.

Your doctor may ask you to give up driving for a little while. After a few weeks, my doctor said that I could drive if it didn't hurt when braking suddenly. Don't lift anything heavier than your babies, which means you may need to only carry one at a time. Plan to spend the first month at home since simply putting car seats into your car can be a challenge. The last thing you want is to open your stitches.

Sex is a no-no. Exercise beyond gentle walking is a no-no. Your doctor may even ask you to hold off on taking any baths. Infections are the devil. This was the hardest for me, since taking my stomach binding off was hardest if I needed to stand. I ended up sitting in the tub with the shower on. I read on the Internet once that the stomach binding can help reduce your uterus size faster. With your stomach muscles turned to jelly, the extra support is really necessary. The longer you use it, the better.

You will start losing weight, fast. Don't be surprised if you have to pee like crazy. Even though your water retention is decreasing, you may still have swollen joints and/or appendages. Hopefully this will be gone by your follow-up appointment. My ankle swelled almost every day for seven months, but it did eventually go away.

If there's any sign of infection on any part of your part, call your doctor. If you have a fever, feel faint or dizzy, or vomit, call your doctor. If you are concerned about anything at all, call your doctor. Calling your doctor is never a wrong answer.

Welcome to Earth

I f this was your first pregnancy, you may be shocked that the hospital let you walk outside with, not one, but TWO human beings. Don't they know that you have no idea what you're doing?! Yes, they know. They're confident that you'll figure it out. The joke's on them, though. Your kids are going to be 18 years old, and you STILL won't have a clue. So, you load into the car and arrive home safely…Now what? Absolutely nothing. Babies are pretty useless in the first three months. This time period has been labeled "the fourth trimester" by Dr. Harvey Karp because babies would gladly stay snuggled in your womb. They sleep, they poop, they eat. Oh, and they cry. And cry. And cry. That's okay, though. A crying baby has a silver lining – it means they trust you. They trust you to come get them when they're upset. You're forming a bond, whoopee! Speaking of bonds, you may notice that your twins seem to know each other. From day one, our twins loved holding hands. It was the most adorable thing I've ever seen. Just thinking about that is enough to get my ovaries going again. Okay, enough of that. Let's get started.

Go Get the Chloroform

I've been told that babies are supposed to sleep a lot during their first three months. Your babies could possibly sleep up to 17 hours per day. The catch is that they don't sleep for more than 2-3 hours at a time because their tiny stomachs constantly need food. My babies, always the exception, had hardcore FOMO. What's FOMO, you ask? "Fear of Missing Out." This millennial garbage means that my babies fought sleep at all hours of the day. They wouldn't nap for more than 30 minutes (unless you were holding them). Once they woke up at night, it took longer to get them to go back to sleep than it did to feed and change them. My boys didn't want to miss out on anything. Your babies will be different, though. No two babies are exactly the same, even identical twins. Let your babies set their own sleep schedule. An adult sleep cycle can last up to two hours, whereas an infant's sleep cycle is roughly 50 minutes.

They do what they want, when they want. You won't succeed with sleep training at this point. If you're lucky, your babies will sleep at the same time. Mine didn't. That meant I was up all day and most of the night. Luckily, I had help in the mornings and slept for a few hours while someone else manned the battlefield. Your babies also may have their days and nights mixed up. It's a common problem and will correct itself eventually. I learned about a neat trick a few months too late. Getting them to fall asleep is easier if you trick them into shutting their eyes. You can use your finger to trace around their face (eyelids, forehead, trace a line down their nose, etc.). Or, my personal favorite was to put a cloth over their eyes. I'd place a burp rag on the top part of their face and rock them to sleep. Worked like a charm.

The best thing you can do right now is to create a routine. A routine will set sleep cues that tell your babies "MOM NEEDS A BREAK SO SHUT YOUR LITTLE BABY EYES." If you stick to your guns, you could possibly get them on the same sleep schedule. Here are examples of some sleep cues: change their booties; feed them; sing a song; and put them in a dark, quiet room. Bath time is also a great sleep cue. Clean babies are sleepy babies. At this time in their lives, they may not be used to hearing each other cry. Eventually, especially if they share a room, crying won't bother the sleeping twin at all. If you're having issues with the twins waking each other up, consider letting one nap in a separate room. Alternatively, your twins might enjoy sleeping next to each other. They shared a womb for so long that sleeping alone might freak them out. Be aware that you will have to separate them down the line, though. Once they start moving around, it's dangerous to co-sleep. I chose to separate my boys from the get-go, and I believe that it made sleep training easier. We used bassinets at first and moved them into cribs after I was well enough to bend down and pick them up. This was sometime around eight weeks. On the really tough nights, I let them sleep in their swings. It's not recommended, but the alternative was to throw shit off of our apartment balcony in a cathartic rage. I think I chose well. The boys slept, and I kept my sanity... I think.

I also let the lowest common denominator rule. That meant that our pace was set by the first twin who wanted something. When one boy was hungry, they both ate. When one boy was tired, we tried to put them both to sleep (emphasis on the 'tried'). The only time this rule didn't apply was when the boys woke up from naps. I did not wake the other twin. Most of the time, they woke each other up, anyway. Nighttime was a different story. If you don't wake the other baby, you most likely will be up again in another hour. It was easier for me to be up twice as long than to get up and down, over and over. Here are a few suggestions for how to handle night feedings:

- Tag team option one: Let your partner handle diaper changes and putting them back to sleep after you feed them.
- Tag team option two: Each of you can be assigned a twin. There is one golden rule, though: You get up together and you go back to sleep together. If one of you finishes with your baby first, don't abandon your partner.
- Tag team option three: Take turns. You can handle one shift while your partner takes the next. At least with this strategy you both can get longer stretches of sleep.
- Multitask: Set up the babies so that they eat while you change them (if you're bottle feeding). I was a pro at this. I would put a blanket under their heads, prop their bottles on another blanket on their chest, and change their booties with ease. Except to burp,

I didn't even take them out of their cribs. They also fell back asleep easier with this method. I was able to get this process down to 30 minutes on most nights.

If you take any advice from this book, please adhere to the following: **do not think about going back to sleep.** Once you're up, just accept it. Otherwise, you will lose your freaking mind. It's a lot more peaceful to take things one step at a time. Warm the bottles: check. Change diaper one: check. Change diaper two: check. And so on. You will go back to sleep, eventually. My husband struggled with this at first. Instead of yelling at him for being selfish, I would rub his back and tell him it was going to be okay. Learning to have patience is hard. You'll get there.

Boob Jizz or Fake Fizz?

Breastfeeding. Yikes. This can be a really difficult decision for some moms. You have four options: Breastfeeding on the tit, pumping and feeding through bottles, formula city, or a combo of any of the preceding options. Let's go through the pros and cons:

- Natural breastfeeding pros:
  1. Best way to bond
  2. No prep
  3. No cleanup
  4. You can eat whatever you want (diets are not recommended as they can reduce your supply)
  5. You'll lose weight from burning 20 calories per ounce
  6. Your nipple freaking knows when your baby is sick. Your milk will then change to suit the baby's needs. WHAT?
  7. Hormones in the milk change day and night to help your little ones sleep
  8. Your immune system builds up their immune system
  9. They taste what you taste
  10. No need to carry around extra equipment (except maybe a cover)
  11. If you need a break from people, you can run away to feed the babes
  12. Delays ovulation
  13. Reduced risk for SIDS

- Natural breastfeeding cons:
  1. Your partner misses out on the fun
  2. The responsibility of feeding two babies 24/7 falls on you
  3. Your milk supply may be too low
  4. You won't know how much they're eating
  5. The twins may use you as a pacifier (i.e. want the boob when they're cranky or ready to sleep)
  6. You might only be able to feed one baby at a time, and each feeding lasts 30 minutes
  7. The first few weeks is brutal. It physically hurts because they haven't learned to properly latch. You may get bruised and cracked nipples

- Pumping pros:
  1. Max results for your supply
  2. Babies can be fed at the same time
  3. Your milk builds up their immune system
  4. People can help give the babies their bottles
  5. Your partner can also form a bond when feeding the twins
  6. Hormones in the milk can help babies sleep at night
  7. You have an excuse to break away from people to go pump
  8. You'll still lose weight (in the beginning, I made 50 ounces of milk. You burn 20 calories per ounce, so I was killing 1,000 calories by sitting on my ass)
  9. Delays ovulation
  10. They taste what you taste
  11. You can keep track of how much they eat
  12. Reduced risk for SIDS

- Pumping cons:
  1. Each session takes 30 minutes. In the first few months, it's important to pump every 3 hours or so
  2. Milk won't change if a baby gets sick
  3. You have to clean bottles, nipples, caps, and your pumping equipment
  4. Carrying your pumping equipment with you everywhere is so annoying
  5. It's a pain in the ass when you're not home and need to store pumped milk

- Formula pros:
  1. Less time consuming
  2. No worries about public pumping or breastfeeding
  3. You can keep track of how much they eat

- Formula cons:
  1. Cost
  2. You still have to clean bottles and nipples unless you use the disposable stuff
  3. The twins won't receive your nutrients, which means there's no extra help when they're sick or need to sleep
  4. They will have to build their own immune system
  5. You have to lose weight the old-fashioned way
  6. Your period will come back faster

No matter what you decide, keep snacks on hand. If you're breastfeeding and want to increase your supply, try eating the following: lactation cookies; oats; spinach; and nursing tea. Fertile Goddess Company makes lactation cookie dough ready to bake, ready to die for and available on Amazon.

I had my heart set on natural breastfeeding, at first. My milk didn't come in until six days after the boys were born. At this point, we were home, I didn't know how to get them to latch correctly, and it honestly gave me the willies. The stress of trying to feed two crying babies was too much for me. I chose a combo method of pumping and formula supplements. I liked that I could monitor how much they were eating. We bought a white board and wrote down how much and when each child ate (trust me, this can get chaotic). Newborns eat around 30 ounces of milk or formula per day. During growth spurts (there's several in the first three months), they'll eat even more. At first, I made enough to feed both kids and then some. Once they started eating more, my backup supply was devoured, and I was barely keeping up. Over the course of a year, I slowly dropped pumping sessions one by one and increased how much formula they received. Honestly, no matter what you choose, there's no wrong answer. As long as those nuggets are healthy and gaining a proper amount of weight, you're doing everything right.

Ridin' Dirty

Do your kids need baths every day? Nope. Feel free to clean them with a wipe or wet rag and move on. I was a sucker. My kids loved bath time so much that we made it a part of their bedtime routine. It was time consuming and tiring, but their stupid little smiles were worth it. There isn't much that's different for twins than just one baby. If you have two baby baths, you could bathe them at the same time. My kids only liked bathing if their baby tubs were in the big tub. It was warmer. Since I could only fit one baby tub in there, I didn't bathe them simultaneously. You could also rotate bath nights and bathe one per night. Maybe your partner could bathe Baby A on certain nights and you bathe Baby B on other nights? Do what works for you. My advice is to make sure you prep before putting them in the water. You'll need towels, soap and lotion. Good luck, comrade.

Should You Ask for Help?

I barely made it through these months. I had no idea what I was doing, I wasn't sleeping, and I didn't have time to do anything except be a mom. My husband went back to working 80-hour weeks right after the boys were born. I volunteered to get up with our children at night so that he could get his beauty sleep. I'm not a martyr, though. My grandmother came to live with us and helped me out. So, even though I didn't sleep for more than a few hours at a time, she was there to give me a break. When I needed to pump, she entertained the troops. When the laundry piled up, she threw it in the wash. When I needed to feed myself, she cooked. You may not be able to get live-in help. However, I can totally understand it if you want the struggle. There were weeks that my grandmother left, and it was just me, the dogs, and the babies. I rarely asked for help during those times because I wanted to learn. I needed to know how to handle my kids alone. How else was I going to get good at this mom thing? My husband was not alone with our kids until several months in. He always asked his parents to come over, and that annoyed me a great deal. It made it very hard to trust him to babysit. It is perfectly acceptable to ask for assistance; it just bothered me that he did it 100% of the time. I know, I know. Men just aren't as good as women.

You can do it all, but you shouldn't have to. You are going to be tired, stressed and recovering from major surgery. You need to bring your A-game to care for those kiddos. Caring for yourself means that you will be better at caring for them. Nobody is going to think that you're a bad mom for requesting help. It's understandable, reasonable and expected. One kid is hard enough. You are a supermom, and superheroes have sidekicks, too. Nobody does it alone.

Space

In these first three months, you don't need a lot of living space. My husband and I stayed in an apartment just fine. You can let your babies sleep in smaller bassinets in your bedroom, or even put them in the same crib (temporarily). Those mother fussers don't move around much at this point. I recommend having a swing, but you could also buy a bassinet that rocks if the swing doesn't work with your budget or living area. For me, the hardest thing about apartment life was taking care of our dogs. Walking them three or four times a day was a pain in the ass. Each walk was at least 15 minutes, usually more, so I was spending around an hour every day taking care of my fur babies. As annoying as this was, the silver lining is that I was exercising. In the beginning, I worried that crying babies would bother our neighbors. We never heard about any complaining, so I'm assuming it was fine. If you're stressed about it, do what makes you comfortable. Get help to move or sign a shorter lease. Everything about babies is trial and error, so you may end up liking where you are, or you may burn the place down. Decisions, decisions.

Four-Letter S Word

SIDS: Sudden Infant Death Syndrome. SIDS is a term used for unexplained baby deaths in the first year of life, usually occurring during sleep. Terrifying, right? You may have heard that premature babies, which twins commonly are, are at a higher risk for SIDS. Well, have no fear. There are things you can do to mitigate this risk.

Since 1994, the "safe to sleep" campaign (formerly known as the "back to sleep" campaign) has seen the rate of SIDS drop steadily. Simply put, you lay your child on his or her back during all sleep times. Don't put anything in their crib or bassinet, and don't lay your children on their sides. I struggled with this campaign since I lived with my grandmother, who always wanted to include a blanket and put the boys on their tummies or sides. Anything in their sleep area is a choking hazard. Children who lay on their sides are more likely to roll onto their stomachs. At this age, if their airway is restricted in any capacity, they can't do anything about it. Suffocation is a major threat. Don't worry about your babies choking on their spit up. Anything they regurgitate is liquid, and they will be able to swallow it. Your kids may develop a flat head from laying on it so much, but that's okay. Tummy time will help get those heads back in shape.

Pacifiers are also beneficial. If the kid is sucking on a binky, it's harder for him to shove his face into the mattress or blanket. Some studies say that pacifiers reduce the risk of SIDS by 90%.

Share a room during the first six months. Babies are at a higher risk in the first half year of life. By sharing a room, you can respond quickly to any sounds of choking or moving around.

Prevent the kids from overheating. Over-bundling can make your twins too warm. Babies aren't good at regulating their own body temperature, so there's not much that they can do if they get hot. The recommended room temperature is 70 degrees Fahrenheit. Dress your babies appropriately, with no blanket. You can use swaddles, though. One of the cutest freaking things is swaddling a newborn and watching him or her suck on their binky. Those baby burritos will melt your heart.

Breastfeeding (or pumping) can provide your twins with much needed antibodies in their first few months of life. Some studies quote a 60% reduction in the risk of SIDS. Boobies are wonderful.

Follow these guidelines. SIDS is scary and you want to take every precaution. I remember checking on my twins several times a night. If their dad checked on them, I always asked if they were breathing. I'll probably keep asking that until the day I die. Even if they're 50 years old, they better answer my call at 1 a.m. or I'm jumping on the first plane to make sure they're okay. Try me.

Milestones

One of the coolest things is watching your kids go from totally useless to amazingly talented. The first time one of my boys put a binky back in his mouth (by himself!), I completely lost my shit. Harvard is going to be expensive. Here are some milestones in the first three months:

- Neck control: Raising his/her head and chest during tummy time
- Hand control: Grabbing toys or reaching for dangling objects
- Smiling (on purpose)
- Babbling
- Looking at faces
- Using different facial expressions

Don't freak out if your kids haven't mastered these skills. They may cross the finish line together, or they might learn at completely different paces. My twins were usually a few days apart in learning new things, and neither of them became interested in grabbing toys until about four months. There are apps that can guide you through expected milestones. My personal favorite is Kinedu. Kinedu has activity plans and a large milestone checklist for each month. You can create a profile for each twin and Kinedu will develop a detailed activity plan for any skills that need work. You kids and your new-age parenting tools.

If you're looking for fun twin activities, try placing them on their stomachs facing each other. You can put a small pillow under their chest to give them leverage. They will practice neck control while talking to their sibling. If they hate tummy time, try putting them side by side under a baby gym. They can reach for dangling toys together.

Now that your giggle monsters are really paying attention to things, have you wondered about screen time? How much TV is too much? According to the American Academy of Pediatrics, it's best to limit screen time for all ages. Children under two years old especially need hands-on interaction to learn with each of the five senses. Excessive screen time can lead to developmental delays, less sleep, and poor-quality family time. It's best to keep screens turned onto educational programs. Even so, kids have a difficult time turning screen education into an understanding about the world. Adult interaction is still needed. One of my kids' favorite shows is *Dave & Ava* on YouTube. There's a surplus of educational videos about colors, numbers, ABCs, shapes, and nursery rhymes. I usually only turn the TV on while they're drinking their bottles. Otherwise, I can't get them to sit still long enough to finish. I also like to interact with them by talking about what's going on in the video. When there's a song about colors, I find objects nearby with the corresponding color and present it to the boys. The TV remains off for the rest of the day. Whatever you decide to do, try to interact with your twins as much as possible. Screens can't provide the same kind of warmth that you do.

General Advice

There's a lot to know about babies, and not just twins specifically.

First off, it's okay to think your babies are ugly. If they were born premature, they didn't get as much time as other babies to build enough cute baby fat. They'll get there.

Next, diaper rashes are super common for newborns. My babies had it bad. In the end, the only thing that worked for us was using Desitin to prevent the rash and Milk of Magnesia to alleviate the symptoms. Milk of Magnesia was not recommended by a doctor. We dabbed a little bit of the liquid onto their rash, let it dry, and put on a new diaper. Any redness was significantly reduced. This may or may not work for you; every baby is different. We found out later that it was a dietary cause. My kiddos have an acid sensitivity, so things like fruit and yogurt made their poop turn into lava. Hopefully you don't have to deal with rashes at all.

In the first month, expect to change roughly ten diapers daily per kid. For you, that's 20 diapers per day. Dayum. After the first month, the frequency will decrease to about eight diapers per day, per kid. That's still a lot of diapers. Don't change a sleeping baby unless you absolutely have to. Poopy diapers should be changed ASAP. After the first month, don't be surprised if your kids don't poop every day.

You need to consider crying a background noise. Go through your checklist: are they hungry, tired, dirty/wet, cold or hot? No? Then they're okay. If you've done everything you can and they're still crying, don't stress. Sometimes babies just need to cry. They could have gas, be over-tired, or just simply want your attention. If you're really concerned, you can ask your doctor about colic. Colic is a diagnosis applied in rules of three: a healthy infant who cries more than three hours a day, more than three days a week, for more than three weeks.

Cultivate your relationship with your partner. Yes, the babies are important, but so is your loved one. Even if it's a small amount of time per day, create some quality time. Talk about things besides the kids. Like, what's on your bucket list? What vacations would you like to take? Any opinions on Donald Trump? Why did Jennifer Lawrence have so many nudes?

We need to talk about social media. You are about to experience something that your parents and grandparents never had to go through. How much should you share online? What information should you keep private? How do you keep other people from sharing too much? Unfortunately, internet etiquette isn't common knowledge. My husband and I decided to keep their names and birthdays from social media, but we couldn't stop other people from sharing. We didn't want their birthdays common knowledge simply because they may use their birthdays as passwords in the future. Hopefully I will raise them better than that, but who knows. Here's something I'm still struggling with: how many pictures and videos should I spread around? My father-in-law, bless his heart, created a shared Google drive for everybody and their dog to be a part of. Now, I already had a private Google drive for the good pictures. I even organized it so that I would know which twin was in each picture. The shared drive was great for family who lived in another state. However, I found myself hesitating to upload anything that I took. I didn't know why at first, and it took me 11 months to suss it out. Those moments are my own private moments with my kids. Yes, I shared them on Instagram with my friends and family, but my account was locked down and nobody could take that content and make it their own. Unless, of course, somebody took a screenshot and posted it themselves. I knew who I was sharing my content with. Each "friend" was vetted, and I had regular contact with them in real life. Most of the time, I posted things to my Instagram story, and it disappeared in 24 hours. By uploading those photos and videos to a shared drive, anybody could download the content and share it with their friends, family and total strangers who seemed familiar but nobody quite knows. Maybe that's the aunt that stopped coming to the reunion when great Uncle Mark died? Yeah, that must be her. So, what can you do? Not a whole lot. I reviewed anything that was posted to that shared drive. Most of the time, everything was fine. I once asked someone to remove naked bath time photos, but that was it. I understand that a part of my hesitation is a selfish desire to keep those moments to myself. I'm a private person. I don't have a Facebook. I don't believe in sharing every single thought you've ever had. This is my special time with my kids. I don't feel like sharing it with the world. In the end, I didn't stress about it too much. My husband kept track of Facebook posts, and that's about it. You really don't have that much control. I know, it sucks.

Babies fall. You get too confident when leaving them on the couch, changing station, etc. and BAM! They roll for the first time. It happens to everyone. I mean, not me, of course. A friend told me about it. I would never accidentally turn my head for a fraction of a section and let one twin plunge two feet onto carpet from the couch. Nope. I never had to call the doctor, who couldn't even understand what I was saying between both me and the baby crying. What, you don't believe me? Well, hypothetically, if that did happen, the baby was totally fine. They're more resilient than they seem. If it happens to you, stay calm (pfft). Call your doctor and look out for any changes in behavior. It's no longer recommended to keep them awake to watch for a concussion. Anyone with a concussion needs sleep to recover. If your baby is excessively sleepy, go to Urgent Care.

Have you ever been given advice that has no scientific backing whatsoever? It's called mom science. Moms have this habit of forming opinions and stating them as fact. You'll especially hear mom science during a pregnancy. "Boys are on purpose; girls are an accident." Wow, how rude. I know plenty of girls who were conceived on purpose and boys on accident. Here's one about newborns: "You shouldn't constantly pick up a crying baby." Oh, hell no. A newborn isn't even old enough to understand what spoiling is. It's crucial to establish a trusting bond between you and your newborns. When a baby this young cries, it's because they need something. Don't let "well, this is the way my grandmother raised her kids" be a reason to withdraw affection. That's not science. It's annoying.

The first three months are the hardest. You're almost done, though. You will sleep again; just not right now. It's incredibly important for you to take care of yourself. Sleep deprivation is a serious issue. It affects both your body and mind. Reaction times are slowed. Double tasking becomes difficult. Even your memory is negatively affected. Sleep deprivation is often used as a torture technique. Accept help when you can, and don't feel bad about needing assistance. The worst is almost over. Pretty soon, those precious little piglets are going to start moving around. Are you ready?

They See Me Rollin'

You Made It!

The worst is over. How does it feel to be on the other side? Was it a sprint, light jog, or an obstacle course with knives? Things are about to get interesting. Their little personalities are going to emerge! Are they happy, shy, brave? You'll soon find out. If you have identical twins, they may start to look different from each other (if they don't already). I was lucky. One of my boys was born with a cowlick. Other than that, I could tell their identities by their head shape. There were other, more subtle clues, like birthmarks, but the general population knew the kids by whether or not there was a cowlick. I enjoyed dressing them alike, hiding the cowlick, and seeing who could guess right. It's the little things that make life exciting.

Your twins are interacting a lot. It's almost as if they've never been apart for their whole lives. Baby conversations are a real thing, people. When my little ones talked to each other, I just assumed they were making yo mama jokes. It may just be a series of strange noises to you, but those kids are bonding for life. They'll always have someone to talk to. My boys were competitive; once one started something new, the other would follow. At first, it was learning how to roll. Then, it was who could say "mama" more. Now, it's who can stuff the most toys into their mouth. I'm so proud.

Milestones

Things are getting fun! Your twins are going to do new things almost every day (or so it seems). They may learn something new and then forget about it for another month. Let's see what you can expect during this time:

- Rolling over: tummy to back is easier than back to tummy
- Laughing!

- Playing with people and toys
- Responding differently to family vs. strangers
- Holding arms up to be carried
- Seeing and playing with his/her reflections
- Recognizing his/her name
- Pushing upper body when lying on tummy
- Reaching for objects while lying on tummy
- Using legs to push forward while lying on tummy
- Pulling objects closer

Take lots of pictures, because they're going to look so different from their newborn phase. Pretty soon they're going to be filing their own taxes. I'm not crying; you're crying.

What kind of activities can your twins do together? Lots. Keep up with tummy time and let them chat together. I bought a fun water mat that they could touch and interact with. My twins really got interested in the baby gym around four months. They also LOVED going outside. If you're looking for a change of scenery, put a blanket on the ground and do tummy time outside. Mirrors are also entertaining. You can buy a small, baby-safe mirror for each twin or let them share one. Sharing one may cause fights, though. I remember doing toy rotations throughout the day. One baby would be in a jumper and the other in a stationary chair saucer. After about 15 minutes, I'd switch them. Sometimes, I'd keep them close enough to reach for the other child's toy. While swinging one baby in the Jumperoo, I'd put the other baby in my lap. They'd both squeal as the swinging twin came close enough to touch. To them, it was magical.

Do You Go Back to Work?

So, your three months are up. Some of you have to go back to work for financial reasons. Some of you may have a choice to make. Do you stay at home, or go back to work? The decision isn't always easy.

Let's talk about the pros of going back to work. For starters, you get a break from the kids. Twins are *hard*. They're hard on your mind, your body, and your soul. It's okay to want to be around adults for part of the day. You also get a paycheck again. However, going back to work may be more difficult than you realize. If you don't have a free nanny, daycare can break the bank. Plus, your mornings and evenings will be frantic. Getting ready, doing drop-offs, pickups, dinner, and bedtime is going to be a sprint. Your work may demand more attention than you can give, especially if overtime is a common occurrence. In my household, my husband works all. the. time. I would have been responsible for everything, every day. Would you continue breastfeeding and pump at work, or would you buy formula? Oh, and prepare for the kids to get sick a lot. Daycare is a cesspool of germs. Did you already use your vacation days for maternity leave? Going back to work comes with its own set of problems.

The choice to stay home was easy for me. The bright side is that I never missed a milestone. I was there for every roll, every word, every step. I also had total control. I knew what they ate, when they ate, and their sleep schedules. My kids and I were tight. The con is that I rarely left my house. I brought the munchkins out for a lunch date occasionally, but going out as the only adult was exhausting. I ordered from Amazon and had my groceries delivered. That kind of lifestyle can drive someone crazy. Believe me, when my husband didn't want to go out for dinner, I was pissed. I ate at home 99% of the time. He got to go out, chat with coworkers, relax and eat his meal without playing patty cake. Let's not forget that taking care of two babies is difficult. You're constantly busy and on your feet. Because of how much my husband worked, I ended up being a housekeeper, as well. All chores fell on my shoulders. I'm not saying that you'll have to deal with that, too, but it's definitely a conversation that you should have with your significant other.

If you're considering staying at home, but you're concerned about re-entering the workforce down the line, let me give you some twin mom resume boosters:

- You're the queen of multitasking
- You have to meet multiple deadlines, every day
- You have to trust your instincts
- Giving up is not an option
- You're used to working under pressure
- There is no work/life balance
- You're always on call
- Teamwork makes the dream work
- You have to anticipate changes and be flexible
- Your patience is astounding
- You're good at making people self sufficient
- You're a pro at prioritizing
- Organization is life
- Working with distractions is a breeze

No matter what you choose, you might feel judged for it. Some women feel like you're not doing enough for feminism if you're a stay-at-home mom. Some women think you're a bad mom for having a career instead. Those women have lost sight of what feminism really is. Having the right to choose is what our grandmothers fought for. Nobody forced you to stay home, and nobody forced you into business. I have a bachelor's, master's, and CPA, yet I hesitate to tell other women that I chose to stay home. It's not like my husband demanded it or that I didn't have a corporate ladder to climb. We shouldn't feel ashamed of either route. Don't let the haters win. It's a wonderful thing to have options!

Sleep Training

The moment you've all been waiting for! Sleep training is the best thing that ever happened to me. Your nuggets should be able to sleep 10-12 hours per night, with maybe one or two feedings. That's so much better than waking up every three hours! Their naps might get better too. Expect three to five hours per day, stretched out over two or three naps. Fuck yeah!

I wish I had known how to sleep train at this age. Unfortunately, I waited until my boogers were eight months old. It was magical. For my next kid (or kids), I'm going to sleep train at three months on the dot. Luckily, you can learn from my mistakes! Here are some methods that you can use:

- Ferber method: Let them cry for a set amount of time. Set your babies in their beds for a nap or bedtime. They should be awake but sleepy. Let them cry for three minutes, then go in and comfort them briefly. Do not pick them up, turn on the light, or offer similar stimulants. Leave the room after a minute. If you can, tag team this strategy with your significant other. You comfort one baby while he (or she) comforts the other. It's fine if you must do it all by yourself – I did. They just get less time with you. Repeat this process again after 5 minutes, then 10, and keep the interval at 10 minutes until the babies are asleep. Do not worry about them crying and keeping each other awake. At this point in their lives, they're used to it. I held off on sleep training because I was afraid of this. Each night, you can increase the crying intervals. I had a hard time with letting them cry past 10 minutes, so I kept it at that and we did just fine. They now fall asleep quickly at naps and bedtime.
- Cry it out: It's exactly what it sounds like. Put your babies in bed and let them have at it. No comforting, no going back in the room. There's some debate about this method. It's unclear if the sudden lack of security can cause psychological or emotional damage.
- Chair method: Grab a seat and sit near them until they fall asleep. Completely ignore them and move your chair farther away each night. This sounds like more of a nightmare for you than for them, but that's just my opinion. It's hard enough to hear them scream in another room, much less a few feet away.
- Wake and sleep: Wake them up slightly after they've already fallen asleep. Get them to fall asleep using your usual method, then do something that will disturb them but not make them open their eyes. They'll fall asleep again in a few seconds, but without you having to rock them or feed them. This teaches them to fall asleep without you.
- Fading: Keep to your usual routine but shorten the length of time. For instance, if you normally rock them to sleep for 30 minutes, cut it down to 20 minutes one night and 10 the next.
- Vary it up: Do something different each night. Rock them to sleep, pat them, sing, let your partner put them to bed, etc. Don't let them get used to (and thus depend on) one bedtime arrangement.

Sleep training should only take a few days to see improvement. If you're being consistent, and it's just not working, try something else. Side note: If you use pacifiers, you will have to repeat sleep training once you're ready to throw those binkies away. Even if you don't pick any of these methods, I highly recommend that you put them to bed at the same time, every day. If you're not sure when that should be, follow their lead. Once one baby starts looking tired, rubbing his/her eyes, getting cranky, etc., start putting them both to sleep. It will be a lot easier on you. Babies love a schedule, don't let anyone tell you different.

There will be times that your kids go through sleep regressions. Naps will be cut short, or they'll wake up earlier. Sleep regression can be caused by teething, growth spurts, sickness, travel, or even learning how to crawl/walk. Don't worry if your wonderful sleepers suddenly turn into night owls. Stick to your usual routine and wait it out.

If you've been swaddling your twins, it's time to end the burrito phase. Once they're moving around, you can either stop swaddling completely or move them into sleep sacks. Your nuggies also need to be in their own beds. If you're worried about separating your babies, putting their cribs next to each other is a good option. It's not recommended to keep them in one crib with a divider. Anything in their beds is a choking hazard, so no blankets, either. Thankfully, the risk of SIDS significantly drops around six months. You can finally breathe.

Remember how I told you that you'd be able to sleep again? This is the time. I think it's ridiculous how negative some people are. "You'll never sleep again!" Sorry, Aunt Judy. I guess my kids are just better than yours.

Food

Those baby birds are still just drinking formula and/or breastmilk. No baby food or solids, yet. Most likely, no rice cereal, either. Prepare to have a fight with some boomers, because rice cereal was something our mothers and grandmothers were told to give. According to "mom science," rice cereal will help your babies sleep longer. It doesn't. In this day and age, it's not recommended because it doesn't provide nutrition. It's a filler and can cause gastrointestinal problems. Plus, your babies are more likely to choke on spit-up after eating something thicker than normal formula or breastmilk. They haven't developed the right muscles and skills to handle thicker substances. So, unless your doctor says otherwise, don't give your babies empty calories. They're doing great by drinking their formula/milk. Believe me, I've been through that fight. Many times. As a matter of fact, it's still going. They've just moved on from rice cereal to other topics. No, Mom! I'm not putting shoes on my kids before they're even walking!

Your babies should be eating 25-30 ounces per day. You've probably noticed that their stomachs are capable of eating more in one sitting, so the frequency of their feedings should decrease. They probably can't hold up their bottles, yet. If you haven't already done so, get a boppy pillow that they can chill in while eating. Prop the bottles on blankets and go do other things (while keeping an eye on them, of course).

How do you know if your kids are eating enough? Proper weight gain, at least four really wet diapers a day, and overall happiness are good indicators. If one child is cranky after breastfeeding, see if he/she will drink some formula as a supplement. Many women choose to stop breastfeeding close to six months. If this is you, that's okay. Breastfeeding can be super stressful, especially if you go back to work. Breastfeeding is wonderfully beneficial if you can keep up with it. Experts have their opinions on how long you should do it, but at the end of the day, they're not the ones who have to spend hours pumping or sitting on the couch. Do what you gotta do.

General Advice

You're going to deal with some new things during this time. Teething may start; the front bottom teeth usually come first. Don't be scared. Put teething rings in the freezer and keep children's Tylenol on hand. Ask your doctor for the proper dosage. If you're not sure if your twins are teething, look for the following: excessive drooling, ear pulling, irritability, decreased appetite, and lots of biting. Teething can hit at any time. One baby may be teething one week, and the other baby the next. It's not fun. Be patient and remember that he/she is hurting. It's easy to get frustrated when you don't know what's going on.

Get ready to talk! If it seems like your twins are listening to you, it's because they are. They may even respond to you once you're done. Their first word could arrive close to six months. Sing to your babies, read books out loud, and tell them about the world. Talk to them while you cook, explain your actions, and point out objects. My husband and I began a word war early on. We battled to make mama or dada their first word. It was a stalemate. One twin said mama, the other said dada. I suppose that was the best possible solution because we're both very sore losers and winners.

Once they know how to move, they'll never stop. Babies love exploring. If you aren't ready to babyproof your home, get a circle baby gate and trap them. In my family, this is known as "The Circle of Trust." They're not going anywhere, and nothing else is getting in. Sorry, doggos.

Okay, so that's it for the 3-6 months phase. Ready for the next? I am!

6-9 MONTHS

Sweet Freedom

love this age. You really start gaining some independence, especially closer to the end of nine months. They're moving around, but you can contain them to the Circle of Trust and get things done around the house. From here on out, I believe twins are easier than one baby. Why? The answer is simple, dear Watson. They entertain each other. You don't have to be the focus. It's brilliant. In between feedings and diaper changes, what would you like to do? Cook a meal for yourself? Paint your nails? Write a book? Go for it.

Milestones

Prepare for total domination. Once they start moving, it never stops. Crawling: check. Walking: check. Taking over the wold: pending. Okay, so they probably aren't going to be walking by nine months. It's coming, though. Lots of moms love the 6-9 range because their children are mobile but not TOO mobile. You don't have to worry about them walking off. Sure, they're almost crawling, but they're not climbing up the fireplace or locking the front door when you go to check the mail. Annoying people will say "It's all over from here!" No, it's actually not. Someone has said that to me for every phase of their life, yet I've loved each phase better than the last. "You'll miss this!" Maybe. It's awesome to see them grow. Let's see what you can look forward to in these three months:

- Looking for hidden or dropped objects
- Learning first words
- Imitating simple actions (like shaking a rattle or waving)
- Dancing to music
- Interacts with familiar people
- Repeating actions that get attention
- Positioning on hands and knees

- Rocking back and forth while on knees
- Scooting
- Sitting up
- Eating solids
- Taking objects out of containers
- Standing firmly when held on legs

Don't be surprised if your twins don't do the standard crawl. There are different types of crawling.

- Bear Crawl: The baby "crawls" with his/her arms and legs straight (booty in the air).
- Army crawl: Belly stays on the floor.
- Boot-scoot boogie: Baby scoots on his/her bottom.
- Crab crawl: The baby moves back or sideways like a crab.
- Rolling: Why do the classic crawl when we can just roll to our destination? It's fun and efficient.

One of my twins is nicknamed "Igor." Even at a year old, he still doesn't do the standard crawl. He drags one leg behind him and scoots it forward as he travels. The best way to help them learn is to put them on their tummies. You can place toys slightly out of reach and give them incentive to move. Sometimes, the best incentive is you. No toy can compare to pulling mom's hair.

Okay, ready for some mom science? Me neither. But 6-9 months is around the time that parents investigate walkers. I mentioned this earlier in the baby shower section, but I'll bring it up again. Walkers do not help a baby learn to walk. They don't develop the right muscles or help kids learn how to balance. If a baby uses a walker a lot, there's a good chance that learning to walk will take longer.

Sitting up was my favorite milestone during this time. We bought a wagon and took them everywhere. They'd just sit and look around. Once crawling became popular, they wanted out of the wagon. This is an awesome age to get out of the house. Even the grocery store was an exciting new venture. We went to festivals, parks, aquariums, and a mini-vacation to New Orleans. Once they know how to sit up, you don't have to be a nazi about burping. Air bubbles naturally come out.

At home, you can experiment with so many different toys. Your twins will love playing with each other. In our home, we have several boxes filled with toys. My boys would go from box to box, pulling everything out. It was amazing to see them stick together. Once the boxes were empty, they'd pull books down from my bookshelf. For family activities, we'd read, sing and play peek-a-boo together. Wrestling was a common occurrence. They loved being flipped upside down. We have a giant bean bag chair in their playroom. Each twin would giggle hysterically as we tossed them onto the bean bag and they rolled down. Kids are awesome.

Sleeping

Things are pretty much the same for their sleep schedule. They should sleep 12 hours per night, with maybe one feeding. If your babies have been taking three naps, it's time to consolidate them into two naps. Sleep training helps with this transition. All in all, your twins could sleep up to 15 hours per day. If you're struggling to get them to go to sleep and STAY asleep, please consider sleep training. My life was so stressful until I bit the bullet. The first few nights may be rough, but you should see improvement in a day or two. I also learned that pacifiers were the cause of our sleep trouble. They completely depended on pacifiers to fall asleep, so when they woke up in the middle of a nap or at night, they'd cry until I put the binky back in their mouth. If it was during a nap, there was no going back to sleep. At six months, the risk of SIDS significantly decreases. You can rest easy.

If you've sleep trained your babies and start seeing some regression, there could be multiple causes. Teething and new milestones are common causes of sleep regression. Don't freak out if they're suddenly not sleeping well. Give it a few days. Try Tylenol and teething toys for teeth pain. Things will most likely go back to normal.

Food

Oh, yeah! It's time for solids! How exciting. When I say solids, I mean pureed baby food. You can make your own or buy jars at the store. At six months, start with one "solid" meal. It doesn't matter what time of day, except I'd try new flavors in the morning to watch for allergic reactions throughout the day. At this point, stick to one flavor every few days. If your twins have a reaction, you need to be able to pinpoint the culprit. Each month, you can add a "solid" meal so that they're eating three meals by nine months. This is in addition to their 25 oz. of formula or milk per day. You've got some hungry, hungry hippos. If your babies handle the pureed food like champs, start giving them "solid-er" foods. Try foods that they can hold and don't need teeth to eat, like bananas and soft carrots. If at first you don't succeed, try again… and again…and again. Sometimes babies need to become familiar with food before they'll accept defeat and eat it. Expect some fake choking, especially at the beginning. They're not used to non-liquid foods, and that first bite of mashed peas is going to be shocking. It takes time to develop their swallowing muscles, so go slow and be patient. If they start sputtering, don't give up. Wait for them to stop and go at it again. Babies can also have about two ounces of water per day now. Sippy cups might be a cool new adventure. Go wild. Get your freak on.

Please Cough in My Face

Now that we're big kids and eating with spoons, what do we do about sharing? Sharing is caring, but it's also the road to germ city. Let's be honest, though: It will be hella stressful on you to keep everything separate. Separate spoons, bottles, sippy cups…what's next? Separate colleges? Not on my watch. Two of everything means twice as many dishes. Plus, all it takes is a shared toy to get the other twin sick. It's going to happen. Just to spite you, they're going to blow raspberries into each other's eyeballs. Then, they're coming after you.

Remember that hand you just pulled out of your daughter's mouth? Yeah, it's going straight into yours. How do germs taste, Mom? My advice: Don't fight it. It's an uphill battle. You might end up putting in more effort to keep them from getting sick than dealing with the actual sickness. Babies can't get the flu shot until they're six months old. It's a two-part system: one shot at six months, then another shot a month later. Let them get sick and build their immune systems.

General Advice

Have your twins started crying around strangers? It's normal. We experienced social anxiety a little early, around four months old. They would cry if we handed them off to "strangers," aka anybody who didn't live in our house. We changed battle tactics. When we arrived at our destination, dad and I would hold them while sitting next to the person who would take them. We'd keep them calm and show the boys that this person was okay with us. After a few minutes, we'd hand them off. It worked like a charm. After a month or two, they didn't have separation anxiety anymore.

Ch-Ch-Ch-Changes!

Is time going by a lightning speed, or do you find yourself impatiently tapping your foot? Many parents look forward to the last three months of baby-dom. My boys just hit twelve months, and we are absolutely loving it. They keep me on my toes, that's for sure. "Babyproofing" never ends. They find new ways to get around old safety tricks. At this point, I gave up trying to stop them from doing bad things. Instead, I started teaching them how to do it right. For instance, when climbing on things like the couch, I taught them that the safest way to get down is butt first. My friends think I'm nuts, but my kids hardly ever hurt themselves. As they learned to walk, I didn't stop them from holding onto unsteady things. It helped them realize how to balance themselves. I was always there, watching, waiting. I think it helps build trust between us too. Kids will be kids; at some point, you have to let them figure things out. Mom won't always be there to keep them out of trouble, and trust me, there will be trouble. Make it double.

Milestones

We're gearing up for the ultimate milestone: the first steps! That's one small step for man, one giant leap for mama. It may take a while, so be patient. It may not even happen by 12 months, and that's okay. I've mentioned it before, and I'll mention it again: shoes aren't necessary. Mom science says shoes will help a child learn to walk. Nuh uh. Shoes are an annoying, cumbersome item of clothing that you don't need to worry about. The best way for a child to learn to walk is by practicing while barefoot. Don't rush it. Once it happens, there's no going back. Enjoy every second of it. There are a lot of other things you can look forward to:

- Imitating words or sounds
- Understanding "no"
- Recognizing names of people or objects

- Comprehending small phrases, like "Where's the dog?"
- Searching for toys
- Copying gestures (i.e. waving or clapping)
- Helping to dress himself/herself by holding out a limb
- Doing donuts while sitting
- Crawling
- Climbing
- Putting objects into a container
- Properly using toys with wheels
- Standing while holding onto furniture
- Standing without assistance
- Going from sitting to kneeling
- Squatting while standing
- Playing with an object while standing
- Cruising around furniture
- Walking with assistance
- First steps (unassisted)

Always keep your phone on you. You never know when you'll need to take a quick video of a new milestone. Also, keep your house key on you. Once, I walked outside to deal with the garbage. One of my boys reached the bottom door handle and locked me out. Luckily, I had a key on me.

Bath time can be so much fun now. Not only can they sit up and play with water toys, but they can do it together. In our house, bath time is an epic adventure every night. They splash, walk around the tub, and recently started feeding me toys. Okay, that last one might be weird, but I don't mind. They think it's hilarious to feed me a rubber duck and then take it back, over and over. They're also fascinated by running water. We fill cups with water and watch as the water is poured out. We have several cups in the tub because sharing is just not an option. Oh, yes. The jealousy is real, in and out of the bathtub. If one brother has a toy, the other brother needs a toy. Possibly the same toy. We've duplicated several purchases because an object might be too exciting to only have one of. Fighting is very common.

In case you're excited about that "no" milestone, remember that understanding it doesn't mean they'll obey it. Prepare to repeat yourself a million times. They'll stop what they're doing and then immediately do it again. And again. And again.

Reading is so exciting. Almost as exciting as chewing on the books. Biting is going to increase in popularity. My feet hurt every night because I can't sit down. If I sit, my boys want to climb all over me, which would be fine, except they also want to bite me. They bite *hard*. Once their teeth start coming in, you have to gently rub their gums and teeth with a damp washcloth. Those chompers are going to take your fingers out. We also had an issue with our boys biting their crib rails. Paint was chipping off. We had to buy rail covers that tied down. It worked, although it's really annoying to untie them for washing.

Another activity you might like is hide and seek. Get a blanket and cover yourself, your children, or anything else and ask, "Where's blah blah? There it is!" They'll get a kick out of it. I've started leaving blankets around the house so that they can pick up the game whenever they want. One twin is very good at seeking me out, so I'll say, "Where's mommy?" before running to find shelter. He's ecstatic when he finds me. I'm ecstatic to play on my phone while he's busy aimlessly crawling around.

Sleep

Life should be pretty sweet right now. Your babies are probably cruising along at 14 hours of sleep per day, including two naps – one in the morning and one in the afternoon. There's not much change in the 9-12 months range for sleep. Once you're closer to 12 months, you need to think about getting rid of all pacifiers. Prolonged use of a pacifier can negatively affect a child's speech and teeth development. If I just caused you a panic attack, put your head between your knees. The key is to be consistent, little mama. Once you're done, everyone will be better for it. There are different approaches to ripping away the one thing your babies love most:

- Cold turkey: This sooooo did not work for me. I have patience and determination, but my children do too. The screaming was endless.
- Snip it: I'll stand by this one. Cut off the tip of your babies' pacifiers. They can't get proper suckage and just spit it out. My kids handled this method a lot better than going cold turkey. I think it gave them comfort to at least have the pacifier near them, even if it wasn't in their mouths. The first night, it took 45 minutes to go to sleep. Each sleep session after that took less and less time. After a few days, the binky was a thing of the past. My boys slept even better than before. When they had the pacifier, they'd wake up in the middle of the night and cry until I put it back in their little baby pie holes. Once the binky was forgotten, they learned how to comfort themselves back to sleep. Mama has been sleeping like a baby ever since. Well, better than a baby. Eight straight hours is bliss.

There are a few other methods, but they are geared toward older children. Such methods include lying to your kids, pleading with them, and replacing the pacifier with another "comfort" item. Since your twins are too young to understand lying and pleading, those methods are out. Before 12 months, it's not recommended to include any items in the crib, including a blanket. So, another "comfort item" is out too. If you're worried about the sudden change, you can take gradual steps. We started by hiding all pacifiers during "awake" time. Then I didn't give them one in the car (even though they slept in their car seats). Once they were used to only using a binky in their cribs, I snipped the tips.

Be strong. Be brave. Be consistent. If they smell fear, they'll walk all over you.

Food

Yeehaw! Saddle up those highchairs, ladies. Your baby nuggets should be eating breakfast, lunch and dinner (as well as the recommended 25 oz. of breastmilk or formula). Once you hit 11 months, two snacks are thrown in too. It gets very annoying to put them in highchairs for each meal time. I've learned to find snacks that aren't too messy and don't require highchairs. Crackers are great if you don't mind crumbs on your floor. You can also give up to 2 oz. of water per kid. Pureed food is still okay, but let's get wild! Your twins can have anything, except honey (for allergy purposes). Here are some great non-pureed food options:

- Bananas
- Apples (Put slices in the fridge! It's great for teething.)
- Oatmeal
- French fries
- Ground beef
- Macaroni
- Ritz crackers

Common choking hazards include pretzels, popcorn, grapes, and hot dog weenies. Once you're comfortable, try some meat. You can start by dicing the meat into pea-sized bites. Anything's game: chicken, steak, pork, shrimp, etc. I learned quickly that my kids wanted control over their mealtime. Feeding themselves was another wacky adventure to them. Yes, it was messy. I let them have their messiest meal right before bath time. I'd get them naked, strap a bib around their necks, and watch the food massacre. Luckily, I have two dogs to match my two children. Dogs are amazing at cleaning dirty children. I might get a third one for my husband.

Babies don't eat much. Most of the food you prepare will end up on the floor. My boys enjoyed rejecting their own food and stealing whatever was on the other twin's tray. Leftovers are wonderful snacks for later on. It's a hassle to cook each meal, so make a little extra and kill two birds with one stone. During our picky phases, I'd have to wait them out. After sitting in the highchair for a few minutes, they'd realize that I'm not making them anything else. For new food, I'd have to force them to taste it. They usually ate it once they stopped being dramatic. I also had success with pretending to eat their food. They thought it was silly and wanted to copy me. At 12 months, they enjoyed "feeding" me. They were actually just holding things to my mouth and taking it away. I'd act shocked when they ate "my" food. My twins mirrored each other. Once one boy did something, the other was quickly in on it. It made it easier to try new things. At the same time, I had to keep things even. If one twin got a cracker, so did the other. The tantrums are real, people. And hilarious. Have you ever seen a kid's rendition of the Chernobyl meltdown? I have. Why? Because his brother took his drink coaster. Priorities, man.

Your pediatrician will probably recommend that you get rid of bottles by 12 months. Your babies magically transform into toddlers and need whole milk. If you're still naturally breastfeeding, go you! That's amazing. Keep it up and add in whole milk to their diet. Introduce the sippy cup as early as you can, even if they don't drink from it. They need time to learn. Start with a little bit of water. A very good friend of mine had difficulty transitioning to milk because her little girl wasn't familiar with cold drinks. My suggestion is to provide cold water when you can. There are different types of sippy cups, too. Most say they're spill proof, but they're not. In our house, the only cup that lives up to the hype is the Nuk brand. The nipple collapses often, but nothing spills out when my kids inevitably drop it. I started giving them sippy cups at six months. By one year, they were pros and transitioned easily. You can gradually get rid of bottles or go cold turkey. In their last week of baby-dom, I slowly replaced each formula bottle time with milk sippy cup time. The change was slow enough so that I could monitor how well they handled whole milk.

Grocery shopping is still difficult. Even though they're masters at sitting up and standing, there's just not enough room in the cart. Most stores only have baskets with one set of leg holes. If the kids are in the back of the basket, where do your groceries go? And how do you keep the groceries safe from wandering teeth? Some kids go the extra mile and only shop while screaming. What a nightmare. I'm still using a grocery delivery service. It's 100% worth it.

As we tried new foods, those pesky rashes returned. Their poop was literally eating their skin. We went back to using Milk of Magnesia on the red skin, letting it dry, and dabbing Desitin over it. Once again, it worked like a charm. I experimented with different foods and found that certain items made it come back. The ultimate culprits were oranges and sugary yogurt.

Restaurants are fun. I'm not a stickler about germs, so we just wipe down the table and put their food in front of them. Both highchairs and booster seats were fine by 12 months. They absolutely love it. As a Texas family, barbecue is a regular dinner request. The first time we took them to a barbecue joint, they lost their minds. They kept shoving meat into their mouths and bouncing up and down. When they ran out of food, they started stealing mine. We had a big mess to clean up at the end. Lots of food also means lots of poop. I change my boys at least five times a day each, sometimes more if they're insanely poopy. Something disgustingly hilarious came up during this time period for us. When I'd change one poopy boy, the other twin would sneakily steal the dirty diaper and run off with it. I will never forget that shit-eating grin when I'd chase the offending party throughout the house. No, they never literally ate shit. It got on their hands once, though. Bleh.

General Advice

Are you one of those parents that just HAS to throw a huge first birthday party, despite the fact that nobody else really cares and your children won't remember it? Yeah, us too. Well, it was really my husband. I just wanted to have dinner with our immediate family. But no, my socialite husband loves an excuse to host a party. We decided to host the party at a kids' bouncing warehouse place. It was expensive, but there were too many people attending for it to be at our house. Plus, time was limited so we didn't have to open all of the gifts. Isn't that the worst part of a party? Watching someone else open gifts that you, as a guest, don't care about? We also set up a college fund and asked everyone to contribute instead of gifting toys. We still received many gifts, but the boys also have their first semester of college paid for. What a wonderful world.

You will inevitably get asked "So who does what?" in regard to their personalities. My boys are very similar. It's almost as if people are looking for you to say one baby is sporty while the other is posh. I don't like putting my boys in a box. I don't always dress them the same or assign color codes. I want them to be their own person, not a stereotype. As they get older, they need to develop independence from both me and each other. I want them to cultivate their own sense of selves. If they decide that they want to do everything together and like the same things, that's great. But I want them to come to that decision alone. I'm afraid that if I make them follow the same routine and don't push them to be different, then they're going to have a hard time adjusting as adults. They're not going to have the same job or live together forever. They're not going to have the same girlfriend or wife. At the end of the day, if they can stand on their own two feet, I've done my job.

So Long, Farewell!

Your twins are looking more and more like toddlers! At the end of 12 months, you'll be saying goodbye to a lot of things. It's bittersweet. The last year has had its ups and downs, left and rights. Their understanding of the world is gaining traction. There's so much to look forward to, still. I can't wait to explain to them how one baby became two. Since one of them was clearly an accident, I'm going to let them duke it out to decide which one was our oopsie.

I hope this book brought you some peace of mind. Child rearing isn't a cookie-cutter, one-size-fits-all situation. You probably have some battle scars, possibly in the shape of baby teeth. Twins are spectacular. Now that the first year is over, are you ready for round two? Lather, rinse, repeat.

Pregnancy resources:

https://www.verywellfamily.com/causes-of-twins-2447133
https://americanpregnancy.org/multiples/complications/
https://www.hopkinsmedicine.org/health/conditions-and-diseases/twintotwin-transfusion-syndrome-ttts
https://www.investopedia.com/insurance/hsa-vs-fsa/
https://www.twiniversity.com/
https://www.babycenter.com/pregnancy-weight-gain-estimator
https://americanpregnancy.org/pregnancy-health/mercury-levels-in-fish/
https://americanpregnancy.org/pregnancy-complications/listeria/
https://americanpregnancy.org/pregnancy-health/caffeine-intake-during-pregnancy/

Child rearing resources:

https://www.babycenter.com/
https://www.parents.com/baby/twins/caring/
https://safetosleep.nichd.nih.gov/safesleepbasics/SIDS/fastfacts
https://www.scientificamerican.com/article/pacifier-greatly-reduces/
https://www.webmd.com/parenting/baby/news/20110613/breastfeeding-cuts-sids-risk
https://www.sleepfoundation.org/articles/how-your-babys-sleep-cycle-differs-your-own
https://www.health.harvard.edu/blog/parents-dont-use-a-baby-walker-2018092714895
https://pediatrics.aappublications.org/content/138/5/e20162591
https://www.webmd.com/parenting/baby/what-is-colic#1

Author's Note

Courtnie Adair wants to thank her family and friends for supporting her. While many examples and stories are true from her life, she also included experiences from her friends and relatives. She sends a big "Thank you" to her patient mother and loving mother-in-law, both of whom are wonderful grandmothers to the two stars of this book.

Printed in the United States
By Bookmasters